Lest
We
Perish

R.G. Beauchain

Library of Congress Control No. **1-10358982381**

6/10/2021

ISBN: 9798733643557 -

For my mother who loved her country and whose guiding principle throughout her entire life was live and let live ... were it not for each of the Sisters of St Joseph and their God given patience I would not have received the most remarkable education in the world ... and most importantly, were it not for my wife Liz who saved my life, this book would never have been written.

Preface

On November 19, 1863, Abraham Lincoln delivered what has become one of the most famous speeches in history; the Gettysburg Address. It took place at the dedication of the cemetery at Gettysburg, Pennsylvania for the fallen soldiers from the North and South who died fighting each other during the Battle of Gettysburg July 1-3, 1863 and now rest in peace with one another.

It needs to be read slowly.

Four score and seven years ago our fathers brought forth on this continent, a new nation, conceived in Liberty, and dedicated to the proposition that all men are created equal.

Now we are engaged in a great civil war, testing whether that nation, or any nation so conceived and so dedicated, can long endure. We are met on a great battle-field of that war. We have come to dedicate a portion of that field, as a final resting place for those who here that gave their lives that that nation might live. It is altogether fitting and proper that we should do this.

But, in a larger sense, we can not dedicate -- we can not consecrate -- we can not hallow -- this ground. The brave men, living and dead, who struggled here, have consecrated it, far above our poor power to add or detract. The world will little note, nor long remember what we say here, but it can never forget what they did here. It is for us the living, rather, to be dedicated here to the unfinished work which they who fought here have thus far so nobly advanced. It is rather for

us to be here dedicated to the great task remaining before us -- that from these honored dead we take increased devotion to that cause for which they gave the last full measure of devotion -- that we here highly resolve that these dead shall not have died in vain -- that this nation, under God, shall have a new birth of freedom -- and that government of the people, by the people, for the people, shall not perish from the earth.

People from around the world continue to make their way to the Gettysburg Cemetery and battlefield where the soldiers from the North and South fought this epic battle. Some remove their hats in respect for this hallowed ground and some bow their heads to remember all the fallen soldiers that lie beneath the ground. There are cemeteries just like Gettysburg all over the world for those that gave their last measure because the leaders could not or would not resolve their differences. We have too many disagreements, too many cemeteries, and yet, it seems we would rather visit the cemeteries than go to any length to achieve peace and accord with one another until it's too late, and we end up building more cemeteries.

The soldiers from the South fought to maintain slavery and preserve their way of life; the soldiers from the North fought to preserve the Republic. The North and South continue to have their differences to this very day, each trying in their own way and sometimes together to form a more perfect union so that this Republic of ours does not perish from the earth.

Once again though, Americans with opposing opinions on how our democracy and country should look like or be managed are embroiled in another great struggle that has become contentious, acrimonious, hateful, divisive, resentful, and threatens the very fabric of our democracy. One side seems to have fallen under a spell to where they have more or less dismissed the rest of us and the other side is in a state of disbelief not understanding what happened to their fellow Americans. We want to shake them awake, ask them to put their beliefs aside for just a minute, stare into their eyes and embrace one another until we all have tears running down our cheeks.

Sad to say, we are far from that moment. Each side continues to vehemently believe that they are right and hold the moral high ground. Outside dark forces from other nations that want our democracy and global influence to fail are using the internet and other means to promote propaganda and divisiveness to further drive us apart from each other and our allies. President Trump, who has yet to proclaim that he is the president for all of us continues to cultivate ongoing secretive relationships with some of our adversaries. The supporters of the president find no fault with his actions or lack of action which has traumatized the rest of us. Fox News, a network that was established in 1996 by Rupert Murdock, a naturalized citizen, to promote the news with a politically biased slant that favors the ideologies and philosophies of the Republican Party has not helped matters either.

A presidential election is about to take place which will decide who is going to lead our nation going forward, and also determine if we as a nation have the mettle to continue to form a more perfect union and relationship with each other as Abraham Lincoln offered, **"It is for us the living, rather, to be dedicated here to the**

unfinished work which they who fought here have thus far so nobly advanced."

The Pilgrims were fleeing England because they would face imprisonment or death if they continued to practice their version of Christianity which was solely related to the passages in the Bible and not the Church of England which they felt had re-interpreted the bible for their own comfort.

They fled to Holland where they made plans to travel to America where they would be free to practice their beliefs without being punished. They returned to England three years later and boarded a rickety old ship called the Mayflower in Southampton with some others who were going to the new land to establish trading posts. The Pilgrims landed at Plymouth in December 1620 at the beginning of winter and experienced the harshest of weather, sickness, death, Indian attacks, food shortages, and yet they had each other's back and surely did not succumb to feeling sorry for themselves. The contemporary paintings show the Pilgrims having a thanksgiving feast with the Indians and this wasn't the case at all for the Indian tribes viewed the Pilgrims as an existential threat to their whole way of life which was a valid assessment.

The pilgrims that got off the Mayflower in 1620 were tougher than nails ... we owe them a debt of gratitude that can only be repaid by us staying the course which is nowhere near as difficult as it was for them. They boarded a ship with strangers wanting to leave England with hopes they'd find their path in the new land across the sea.

I would like to invite each of you when you begin reading this book to imagine you have just boarded a train going from New York to Los Angeles. The trip is going to take three days which I thought would give each of you time to read the book and ponder what I have written and hoping of course everyone stays on the train. Some of you might wish you hadn't boarded, some will be glad they didn't get off the train in Kansas, and hopefully, some will arrive in LA seeing things in a different light. I apologize if any of my views seemed to be inflammatory or caustic; I meant only to highlight not denigrate.

The narrative will seem to flow in a thought generating pattern rather than in a subject or topical manner ... this was purposeful as I wanted the reader to feel close at hand.

I thought it best to put different parts of history back into play so the reader could have a better perspective of what happened over the last 100 years that got us to where we are today and to show in some degree how each generation is still adversely affected by events from previous generations that haven't had closure or unacceptable endings ... just saying 'It is what it is doesn't remove the itch'.

Chapter 1

I strolled into the kitchen on Wednesday morning, November the 9th, 2016 just as my wife turned away from the kitchen sink and proclaimed in an almost hysterical voice, "Trump won!" …"What!" … "Yes, he won by the electoral votes and Hillary won by the plurality vote." I was struck with disbelief and kept repeating aloud over and over, "No, no, this cannot be … what have we done … oh, my God, this is going to be the worst roller coaster ride of the century … the world is not going to believe what has happened much less understand it!" I could not stop ranting, "… this man is going to disassemble this nation piece by piece, law by law, and principle by principle until it doesn't resemble a democratic republic! He has always hated the way we are and the way this country operates ... he loves autocracies and the despots that run them!"

I soon quieted down and was able to bring the previous month back into focus to where I remembered seeing on TV that the CIA had informed President Obama that they and 17 other international intelligence services had confirmed Russian agents had cyber-attacked their way into some of the U.S. media companies and the DNC (Democratic National Headquarters). They stole strategic campaign plans and salted ads with high profile propaganda to influence the voters. Ten days before the election, Hillary Clinton was still ahead in the polls to win by 10 points, so what could have happened that caused such an upset!?

I personally thought Trump behaved like a rake during the GOP primary debates. I also remembered seeing something odd during his early campaign rallies, like he was on to something. Looking back, I remember thinking to myself one night when I was watching the news coverage on one of his rallies that he seemed to have connected to the crowd at the rally; like when a miner strikes pay dirt. He discovered there was a cross section of the country that was in some way attracted or intrigued by his dark personality, his secretive financial notoriety, his spontaneous vulgarity, or his brash behavior. They loved him when he walked up behind Hillary while she was responding to a question from one of the moderators during one of the debates; he was mocking her. It was clear that this type of behavior endeared his base to where they began to see him as one of them. He began working up his supporters at his rallies, "What am I going to do with her when I'm elected?" and the crowd screamed back, "Lock her up!" and "Who is going to pay for the wall?" and the crowd screamed back, "Mexico!"

There was no doubt in my mind that Trump knew his base had all but turned a blind eye to his outrageous sexual predatorial behavior that was revealed on the video taken during one of his campaign bus rides … his raunchy language, nonstop lies, and demonization of the media for creating what he called fake news continued until he knew he had them hook, line, and sinker. It had all the same apocalyptic similarities of what took place in Jonestown and Waco with no rhyme or reason as well as to why some Americans would turn their nation over to him.

I don't believe anyone, including the Russians, ever thought Trump had a chance to win the 2016 election … but it happened. Seventeen international intelligence sources confirmed that the Russians used Facebook and other media companies to send over 120 million political ads to influence people they believed would be susceptible to the false information. It must've worked and there was no way any of his base would ever admit they had been played by some crazy Russian hackers.

Chapter 2

We of late have been given a lesson on how easy it would be to lose our democracy along with this precious home we call the United States of America and if this doesn't motivate you to want to take a closer look at your part in all of this, then shame on you and shame on us all!

I do not intend to cast any dispersions on those who voted for Donald Trump or Hillary Clinton November 8, 2016, and yet, there was so much controversy over the last four years with respect to the Trump presidency that this exercise will seem to be more about the Trump supporters because the rest of us want more than anything to understand how they all came to the conclusion that Trump was going to make the best president and make this nation great again when we thought it already was great. What did they see or not see that made Trump their choice?

So, let's begin!

What dynamics were in play that drew some of us to decide on Donald Trump and others to Hillary Clinton? The intelligence sector confirmed that the Russians were over the hill involved with sending out over 120 million ads to people they deemed susceptible to their disinformation messaging. The GOP controlled senate continued to insist Hillary Clinton was responsible for the U.S. Embassy in Benghazi being overrun in 2012 by Al-Qaeda. FBI Director Comey made vague accusations right up to ten days before Election Day against Hillary for having used her private email service for her government business. The CIA said the Russians hacked into the Democratic Headquarters and stole Clinton's campaign strategy. For sure, it wasn't a level playing field for Clinton, and yet, the polls had her winning by 10 points.

President Obama announced on TV that the Russians had interfered with our election. The CIA already had pin pointed the location in the U.S. used by a Russian GRU unit to conduct cyber hacks and the disbursement of propaganda ads via Facebook and other U.S. media companies. President Obama should have postponed the election even though there would have been a loud outcry from the right, however, our intelligence services along with those from 17 other countries would have put to rest the backlash with damning evidence that the Trump campaign may have used a foreign government(s) to aid their campaign which is against the law. This did not happen and Trump won the Electoral Vote by the slimmest of margins and the U.S. descended into a quagmire of political discontent. As an aside, you can be sure Trump would have postponed the election in 2020 if something similar had happened on his watch!

Robert Mueller was appointed by Attorney General Jeff Sessions to conduct an inquiry into the election which took two years and ended with Mueller proclaiming there was insufficient evidence to charge the Trump campaign with collusion even though there was overwhelming evidence they may in fact had colluded with the Russians which in of itself was a travesty of our Justice system and shows how Trump had successfully used Jeff Sessions and Rod Rosenstein as his personal legal system.

On several occasions, GOP Congressman Nunes from California who is a member of the Congressional Intelligence Committee made several visits to the WH. He was seen on TV carrying documents to Trump that I'm sure some of the other members of his committee may have objected to for it was obvious they may have been related to the ongoing investigation into the conduct of Trump and his campaign workers during the campaign … wasn't this a criminal act?

To add salt to the wound, the GOP Senate intelligence committee finally announced in early 2020 that there was in fact conclusive evidence that the Russian GRU units had hacked into the DNC Headquarters and used Facebook and other methods to transmit propaganda to the U.S. public during and up to the 2016 election, but failed to make a connection of this to the Trump campaign. Several of the Trump campaign workers had been found guilty of lying to the FBI about their involvement with Julius Assange of Wikileaks and several Russian oligarchs to where Stone and Manafort were now serving prison sentences.

So, what has all of this got to do with the voters? For one, why wasn't there a national outcry from all Americans; there wasn't, which means, as long as some of us got who we wanted into power, the end justified the means. How long does anyone think this democracy is going to last if we all behave this way, or worse, do some of us even care because this is exactly what happens when truth and justice are set aside. When we start giving our candidates or a political party a pass for underhanded behavior, it also means our personal moral compasses have shifted to where we as a nation will soon be severely compromised because we are supposed to be a nation of laws not politics.

Most importantly, the one thing I noticed throughout the entire first two years of Trump's term was the deafening silence from the GOP and the Trump supporters; see no evil hear no evil. This would not have been unusual in Russia, but it was damn sure unusual in America! To this day I feel positive that the Trump voters knew something had happened in the election that was not quite right, and Trump wasted no time reconvening his rallies to put the past behind them, convince his base that the Democrats were on a witch hunt, and that he was their bigger than life president; he just never got around to telling the rest of the country that he was our president too!

What his base didn't know when they stuck their finger in the Trump tar baby was that the spiritual laws of the Universe came into play and before they knew it, they couldn't get their feet or hands unstuck from tar baby Trump as well.

The rest of us however knew something wasn't right because every president's first job in office is to wash away the stinging differences made during the campaign and become the president for all of us; it's what a new president should do, and yet, this never happened because this was just the way Trump wanted the election to turn out; us against them! Trump wanted exclusivity; not inclusivity!

So, how did some of us not see what was coming or worse, even happening? I believe the number one dynamic that came into play in our country was that many of us had a predisposed political investment to a political party that overshadowed our personal values as Americans. I'm from Massachusetts which tends to vote more for Democrats than Republicans, however, there have been numerous occasions when the Democratic candidate for governor did not impress the voters and they opted for the GOP candidate for governor instead. This is the way our founders intended the electoral process to work. We should never have so much of an investment in a political party that it over shadows our moral compass when we are voting for someone who is going to lead us all; having an allegiance to the nation means we must first have an allegiance to each other. We first discern and evaluate the character of the candidate to ensure they have some degree of integrity, humility, kindness, and principles to lead us <u>all</u> forward, not just those in their party. The Declaration of Independence and Constitution made no mention of any political parties which meant we were only meant to debate, argue, and compromise over policies.

We then go through our individual processes to select who we each feels is best for us, but I don't believe we took into account how we are going to get along with each other afterwards; it's always been an all or nothing approach!

It gets worse! I live in a predominantly Republican area and I was blown away to where I couldn't believe a recent article in the local newspaper written by Cynthia Tucker entitled, 'Republicans Hate Democracy'. She quoted GOP Senator Mike Lee from Utah when he tweeted, "We're not a democracy. Democracy isn't the objective; liberty, peace, and prosperity are. We want the human condition to flourish. Rank democracy can thwart that." She went on to quote his fellow GOP defenders who have been saying this for decades now, in fact, from the days of the John Birch Society that was formed in Wisconsin in the 60's that claimed "America is a Democratic Republic" ... Our Declaration of Independence mentions our inalienable rights of life, liberty, and the pursuit of happiness and thank God they didn't use the word money instead of happiness because the two can be light years apart!

The meaning of the word 'rank' in Webster's dictionary implies a putrid, festering, or rancid condition. The GOP at times does seem to have more of an investment in the human condition than it does in our values or moral compass and now we are left to wonder if they have turned a blind eye or are attracted to fascism, autocracy, and authoritarianism as well.

So, there are those who somewhat follow the campaigns, those that do not believe what any politician says, those who are oblivious to the entire process, those that are dedicated to electing candidates from only one party regardless of their candidate's worth, and lastly, we must not forget the 93 million eligible voters who did not show up to vote in the 2016 election! Shame on them! Maybe we should think about fining those who do not vote $100. In the case of the 2016 election this would have amounted to nearly ten billion dollars. This money could then be used to support the campaigns of the presidential candidates during the next presidential election. We could then outlaw PAC funding groups and mandate that candidates running for public office only be allowed to broadcast their policies and their opponent's proven liabilities; unproven personal defamation should never be allowed on television ads. Talk about a breath of fresh air!

Chapter 3

Well that's not what happened … the next four years turned out to be a nonstop psychedelic trip of chaos and incivility. Trump tells the world that he's done more for the U.S. than any other president … this isn't true … he has undone ten times more than he created, in fact, he has methodically and systematically disassembled this Republic in ways that no previous president would have ever envisioned let alone attempted.

The following is a list of policies, bills, rules, or laws that Trump repealed during his first month in office that affect the health, livelihood and pocket books of us all. The question is, what did his voters think this man was going to do for them when he took office, because, until I read the following list, I had no idea how he and his lackeys in his administration were going to take an axe to so many programs and policies that benefitted everyone in main stream America.

So, let's look at the list:

Trump withdrew the U.S. from the Trans-Pacific Partnership coming out of the gate. The trade deal would have established a trade partnership between the United States and 16 countries on the Pacific Rim … China was not included in the partnership and this would've been a bargaining chip down the road in getting China to stop devaluating their currency which undercut the top 20 GDP countries in the marketplace and put an end to their infringement of U.S. copyright and patent protection. To make matters worse, China just signed the world's largest trade deal in the Pacific Rim area, an agreement that involves a market of 2.2 billion people, and we, the United States of America are not in it … so much for President Trump being the great deal maker when he withdrew us from the TPP plan all because it was brokered by Obama. Sad! This is the epitome of stupid is what stupid does!

Revoked a rule that expanded the number of people who could earn overtime pay. This in and of itself needs no further explanation for middle class workers were the losers.

Reversal of a rule that would mandate oil and gas companies to report payments to foreign governments. The Securities and Exchange Commission will no longer receive this information. This means that U.S. companies do not have to conduct their overseas business affairs in an above board manner, in fact, they now can manage their foreign business dealings disingenuously .

Stopped a rule that would require large companies to report worker incomes by race and gender. The rule was aimed at reducing pay disparity.

Reversed an interpretation of the Civil Rights Act that provided protection to transgender workers. We will no longer be trying to understand what it's like to walk in someone else's shoes if we repeal policies like this one.

Ended a rule that barred employers from taking some or all of the tips given to service employees. Can you believe a member of the working middle class being okay with this?

Canceled a rule mandating financial advisers to act in the best interests of their clients. Still with mc!

Ended a rule that allowed consumers to file class-action suits against financial companies. It gets worse!

Ended limits on the ability of states to drug test those seeking unemployment benefits. Whoa!

Reversed a policy that allowed states to develop their own work requirements for welfare recipients. States should manage their own welfare programs.

Revoked an executive order that mandated compliance by contractors with laws protecting women in the workplace. Before the 2014 order, a report found that companies with federal contracts worth millions of dollars had scores of violations of labor and civil rights laws.

Repeal of a rule allowing states to create retirement savings plans for private-sector workers. Who would not have benefitted from this!

Appointed Mick Mulvaney, a fierce opponent of the Consumer Financial Protection Bureau, to serve as its interim leader. Mulvaney once said the Bureau was a "joke." Maybe now it is!

Blocked implementation of a rule that would have made it easier for farmers to sue big agricultural companies. So much for Trump bragging on being the farmer's best friend.

Repeal of a bill that mandated employers maintain records of workplace injuries. This is an integral part of the Osha safety system! Pretty plain why companies with lax safety programs would want this one repealed!

Removed information about worker injuries from the Occupational Safety and Health Administration website. Not safety minded at all!

Killed a rule mandating that government contractors disclose past violations of labor law. More corruption!

Rescinded a President Obama effort to reduce mandatory sentences. Attorney General Jeff Sessions ordered that prosecutors seek the most stringent penalties possible in criminal cases. Please tell me this isn't so! Who pays for this?

Canceled Obama's phaseout of the use of private prisons. Why does the GOP want to incarcerate so many people for so long in commercial prisons? Could it be that it's big business? And of course, the black population of most prisons is 70 percent.

Lawyer Jennifer Robinson said she witnessed Trump associate Charles Johnson and Rep. Dana Rohrabacher meet with Julian Assange in the Ecuadorian Embassy in London to offer Assange a presidential pardon if he would not reveal Russia's involvement in the 2016 hacking of the Democratic Party in August 2017. Is this legal!

Reversed restrictions on providing surplus military gear to police departments. Those restrictions were implemented by the Obama administration after the unrest in Ferguson, Mo. Police departments do not need battlefield equipment, and if they do, they should call in the National Guard! Wannabe soldiers in the police departments should join the Army!

Reversed a ban on civil forfeiture. Law enforcement officials are now once again able to seize assets from suspects who haven't been convicted of any crime. Accusing someone vs convicting someone in a court of law is plain for anyone to see … this violates the very core of our Constitution.

It was right about here when President Trump went to Helsinki and met secretly for two hours with Putin. The world will never forget the looks of the two men when they came out of the meeting to meet with the press … Putin looked like the cat that swallowed the canary and Trump looked like the canary … and everyone in the world had the same impression! We have yet to see or hear anything that was discussed … this so resembles the movie Manchurian Candidate … are we really okay with this?

Reversed the government's position on a voter ID law in Texas. Under the Obama administration, the Justice Department argued that the law had discriminatory intent against many Hispanics who did not have a driver's license. Under Sessions, the Justice Dept. withdrew that complaint and a federal court threw out the law.

Reviewed Justice Department efforts to address problematic police departments. An effort to address concerns in the Baltimore Police Department was delayed. Nothing ventured nothing gained! It's the bad apples and some police unions that want to look innocuous that cast a black mark on the police departments; not the honorable police officers who put their lives on the line for us every day .

Requested a review of the convictions of a Blackwater guard for killings of unarmed Iraqi civilians in 2007. At the time, Blackwater's CEO was Erik Prince, brother of Education Secretary Betsy DeVos. This was overhauled and scaled down by the Department of Justice and the State Department. I need say no more!

In August, Politico reported that some representatives of oil and gas companies are worried that Trump was moving too quickly to reverse regulations on their industry. "You don't need to roll things back so fast that it opens an opportunity for outsiders to criticize or for something bad to happen," One analyst said, "Imagine us acting too quick for the oil companies!"

Withdrew U.S. from the Paris Climate Accords. I'd love to hear some thoughts from some of the folks in the mid-west after all the bad weather they've gone through over the last four years!

Blocked the Clean Power Plan. The plan implemented under Obama focused on reducing greenhouse gas emissions from power plants. The Post reported that the administration would seek to repeal it entirely. Tens of thousands of children with asthma and older folks with COPD are hospitalized every year as a result of coal burning power plants belching out thousands of tons of micro ash particulates, SO_2, and CO_2.

Suspended a rule limiting methane leaks from drilling on federal land. Methane is 80 times a much more potent greenhouse gas than carbon dioxide and is the number one culprit that causes global warming. Is anyone out there listening to this!

Ended a study on the health effects of mountaintop-removal mining. The process involves blasting away the tops of hills and mountains to get at coal seams under the surface. I can only imagine how much methane gas can escape from an entire mountain top!

Rescinded a rule mandating that rising sea levels be considered when building public infrastructure in flood-prone areas. Duh! Is there anyone that is watching the speed with which the ice is melting around the two poles, and especially Antarctica; guess not … another duh moment may soon be coming where we could be scurrying like rats for higher ground!

Reversed an Obama ban on drilling for oil in the Arctic. This is an obscenity with our civilization standing on the precipice of extinction due to our use of fossil fuels!

Announced a reduction in the scale of several national monuments. Trump signed an executive order ordering a review of monuments added in the past 20 years, opening up the possibility that some areas previously set aside would have that status revoked. Last month, Trump announced plans to reduce the size of two, one after lobbying from a uranium company. Destroying our national parks in favor of mining more uranium. Ludicrous! Talk about making it easier for those companies that provide financial political support to the leaders in the swamp to get what they want.

Ignored a deadline to implement a rule regulating smog. C'mon!

Withdrew a rule regulating fracking on public land. We need to say no to the oil companies who will contaminate our water supply and destabilize the earth's crust! Ask the folks in Oklahoma how fracking has affected their well-being!

Announced plans to reconsider controversial protections for the sage grouse in western states. The bird's habitat has been reduced as sagebrush has been removed in places that are being developed, often for oil and gas drilling. While not officially endangered, conservation groups worry about the sage grouse's fate. As we all should! Everyone should see the documentary by David Attenborough on what will happen if we don't properly manage the wildlife on our planet.

Postponed an EPA rule that would have let chemical plants better evaluate and inform the public about possible safety issues. This decision, made in June, drew new attention after Hurricane Harvey flooding led to an explosion at a facility near Houston. This is another case of letting the foxes guard the hen house!

Rejected a proposed ban on the pesticide chlorpyrifos. The month after this decision, a group of farmworkers were sickened by exposure to the chemical.

Reversed a ban on plastic bottles at national parks. Say this isn't so!

Repealed a ban on lead bullets. The bullets were banned under Obama because the lead can poison wildlife.

Rescinded a limit on the number of sea animals that can be trapped or killed in unattended fishing nets. When will we learn to be at one with wildlife?

Delayed and potentially rolled back automotive fuel efficiency standards. This was the worst when we should be doing everything within our power to roll back conditions that promote negative climate change! CO_2 levels dropped significantly during 2020 due to quarantining people during the Covid virus.

Began repeal of a rule that would weaken emissions standards for some truck components. Say this isn't so!

Repealed the Waters of the United States rule. This rule expanded the definition of water bodies that were protected by the Environmental Protection Agency.

Ended a rule banning dumping waste from mining into streams. Bet you didn't know about this one! Worse than disgusting.

Reversed a rule banning hunting bears and wolves. The ban applied to federal refuges in Alaska and prohibited hunting predators using bait and certain hunting methods.

Repealed a bi-partisan amendment that prohibited the government from seizing private land for federal use! Are you sure this wasn't in Russia?

Removed more than a dozen academics from the EPA's Scientific Advisory Board. Now why would they go and do this?

Removed a bike-sharing station at the White House. This surely sets the tone for those working in the WH!

Intends to decertify the landmark agreement with Iran aimed at limiting that nation's ability to develop nuclear weapons. Such a declaration would force Congress to decide whether sanctions should again be imposed on Iran. This is nothing more than payback for the 51 U.S. hostages that were kidnapped from our embassy in 1979 and it's not going to go away until they get what they want; war! Most Americans do not know why all this happened … it happened when the U.S. CIA conducted a black op mission, named TPAJAX in 1953 on behalf of the UK that ended with the U.S. CIA arranging the overthrow of the democratically elected Prime

Minister Mahammad Mossadegh? … and now you know the rest of the story!

Plans to phase out a policy for people who immigrated to the U.S. illegally as children so they could now work legally and avoid deportation failed. The program, begun under Obama, is called Deferred Action for Childhood Arrivals or DACA.

Cut the number of migrants and refugees allowed from seven predominantly Muslim countries. Not who we are or what we are about!

Ended "temporary protected status" designations for tens of thousands of Central Americans and Haitians seeking refuge in the U.S. This is unfinished business that needs bi-partisan closure.

Proposed revoking a rule that allowed the spouses of those with H-1B visas to work in the U.S.

Ended a process that made it easier for people to extend H-1B visas for most of the year.

Ended a State Department office that oversaw international sanctions. The administration has not met an Oct. 1 deadline to implement new sanctions on Russia. Another duh! Remember Helsinki? Russia sent 10 spies (that we know of) to gather and collect information on our nuclear weapons programs who were monitored by the FBI from the time they landed here in 2002 until they were all seized in 2010. The idea that tens of millions of Americans have no idea whatsoever of how great a threat Putin can be in today's times is incomprehensible! If Putin thought for a second that he could successfully launch a sneak attack against us and suffer minimal retaliation, he would do so in a heartbeat. Americans need to get real … grow up … read!!

Repealed a rule allowing transgender individuals to serve in the military. The measure is currently being considered in the courts.

Stopped funding some UN relief efforts. Instead, the administration will back efforts by private organizations and faith-based groups.

Pulled out of the UN's Global Compact on Migration. The concern, according to Secretary of State Rex Tillerson, was that it "could undermine the sovereign right of the United States to enforce our immigration laws and secure our borders." Valid supposition, however, we are all descendants of immigrants … all of us!

Rolled back Obama's 'Outreach to Cuba.' This is almost identical to the Iran situation. Ever wonder why the GOP would never open normal relations with Cuba? Castro detested American businesses and the Mafia for propping up the Cuban dictator Baptista so they could take advantage of cheap Cuban labor and entice Cuban women to work in their own private whore houses. Castro knew it would only be a matter of time before the U.S. invaded Cuba; he was right! A volume could be written about this Cuban and American tragedy. We can thank JFK for standing his ground and not giving in to the wishes of the Republican Party, the CIA, and the Joint Chiefs! But we need to ask a bigger question: Why was the GOP so eager to invite China into the circle of trusted allies in the UN when they had been instrumental in killing over 30,000 U.S. troops in North Korea? Money! To my knowledge, other than the Bay of Pigs Invasion, Cuba has not killed one American!

Ended the Deferred Action for Parents of Americans and Lawful Permanent Residents program. DAPA extended protections for some immigrant parents whose children were citizens of or residents in the United States. This is so sad and ugly!

Reversed a policy instituted by the Obama administration to expand punishments for campus sexual assaults. Parents with daughters should be livid that their daughters will not be safe on campus because young male predators know they will not be caught let alone prosecuted because of this policy being repealed by a president who is an accused sexual predator himself and who has multiple forced sexual indictments awaiting him when his term of president is over.

Repealed 72 documents defining the rights of students with disabilities. The administration argues that this won't affect how those students are educated. They really did strip 72 documents that gave students with disabilities a leg up!

Rolled back school lunch standards championed by Michelle Obama.

Withdrew federal protections for transgender students in schools. Under the rule approved by Obama, transgender students could use school bathrooms that corresponded to their current gender identities. GOP members need to walk in their shoes.

Canceled a partnership with the Consumer Financial Protection Bureau aimed at policing student loan fraud. How do we rectify this type of reasoning?

Reversed a rule that mandated how achievement is measured in schools … and we still have not created an all encompassing rule to grade our students … 19 of 20 top GDP countries in the world have done so … not interested in all American students being smart; just a few … a very select few!

Repealed a rule mandating certain requirements for teacher-preparation programs. Now why would anyone not want to have teachers that are better prepared?

Reversed a rule that would ban gun sales to those deemed "mentally defective" by the government. Are you still with me! Everyone that wants to carry or transport a firearm away from their dwelling should require a permit and/or should undergo an MMPI test to insure they have the mental capacity to do so safely before they can even purchase and drive home with a gun.

Reconsidered a ban on carrying firearms on Army Corps of Engineers land.

Narrowed the definition of "fugitive" to reduce the number of people not allowed to own guns. Sleezy at best!

Halted or canceled hundreds of other minor regulatory actions.

Ended payments to insurers meant to expand health-care coverage for low-income Americans. Another ongoing American tragedy!

Erased net neutrality rules established by the FCC under Obama. The rules prevented internet service providers from charging more for certain types of internet traffic bearing in mind the internet was a gift to the world from the USA with the idea it would always be unregulated, unowned, and free. More about Americans not reading and being asleep at the wheel!

Repealed a rule mandating that Internet service providers seek permission before selling personal information. Getting overwhelmed yet!

Revoked a ban on denying funding for Planned Parenthood at the state level. This is a disgrace in and of itself … every woman should have dominion over their own body!!!! This includes being able to have an abortion. Government should not have the right to mandate otherwise; Pro Life compels wherein Pro Choice chooses … it's quite simple to see the difference!

Revoked an Obama rule barring those who'd served as registered lobbyists the prior year from taking jobs with the administration. This was a great rule in preventing lobbyists from expanding their territory any further into the workings of our government. Lobbyists should be forbidden to have any contact with any government leaders whatsoever!

Determined that claims of violations of religious freedom would trump protections for gay and transgender people. This is the cake-for-a-gay-wedding issue; the Trump Justice Department takes the position that the religious beliefs of a business owner can take precedence over the civil rights of employees or customers. What would be the next reason the GOP wouldn't want to sell you something?

Began the process of undoing the Johnson Amendment. The law bars religious institutions from taking positions on political candidates. An effort to include this repeal in a tax reform package ended without success. Yippee!

Scrapped an Obama-era rule requiring that airlines disclose baggage fees. More about the GOP working for big business than the customers that make big business possible! Makes me wonder why we would want to give the airlines some Covid financial relief when they're never thinking about relief for us and that's a long list!

Reversed a policy aimed at reducing mortgage insurance premiums for new FHA loans. You must be sitting down by now.

Cut outreach aimed at bolstering enrollment in Obamacare. Again, we stand mute until it's too late!

Limited the Obamacare mandate that birth control be covered in health-care plans. The administration will give employers and insurers the right to exempt such coverage on religious or moral grounds.

Slow or nonexistent staffing at the Senate-confirmed along with management levels across administration agencies. Snail progress is how nothing gets done that they don't want done.

Repealed a rule mandating consolidation of transit planning authorities. There are 490 MPO's (Municipal Planning Organizations) that interface with the big gears of government to ensure we don't get trampled on by those that don't really give a damn about what happens in your area. Not anymore! Feel better?

Ended the declaration of June as Pride Month and the practice of recognizing the end of Ramadan with an iftar dinner. This shows their true colors! Get it? True colors!

Canceled public reporting on visitors to the White House and other online data. I can sure understand why they'd want this one repealed! For sure they don't want us to know all the folks they've invited into the WH; were the Russians in the Oval Room and exclamation point?

Towards the end of President Trump's third year in office, the U.S. Senate found him not guilty of having committed an impeachable offense as charged by Congress for having withheld funds ($400MM) authorized by Congress to Ukraine to purchase weapons to be used in their ongoing fight against the Russians in order to force the President of Ukraine to initiate an investigation against Joe Biden and his son to darken Joe Biden's chances in next year's election.

There was overwhelming evidence produced by distinguished State Department diplomats, ambassadors, and duty bound U.S. military officers that had no affect whatsoever on the GOP led Senate. For sure, if Hillary had won and she had asked the Ukraine president to investigate the GOP opponent for the 2030 election, she would have been found guilty, drawn, and quartered. The GOP conducted 17 hearings on her that ended with her having no complicity in the Benghazi attacks. Justice depends on who and which party is in power! How are we ever going to have justice in our land when some of our elected officials will not set politics and their constituents aside to faithfully execute their <u>constitutional duties</u> with honor because if we cannot do this then we have nothing and will have failed as a democracy. Duty, honor, and country is the creed for all members in the armed forces, and this also should include our senators, congressional representatives, and our president! They are our servants not our masters!

Chapter 4

This infamous quote from Nikita Khruschev, Premiere of Soviet Russia from 1958-64; "We do not have to invade the United States; we will destroy you from within" came front and center when I sat down to watch the nightly news in May of 2017. There was president Trump entertaining the Russian ambassador with his entire Russian entourage of attachés in the Oval Room via Russia state sponsored TV. Did his supporters or the GOP not think there was anything at all wrong with Russian state media TV crews in the WH? Did they not think it odd that none of our national television networks had not been invited? The rest of us were speechless! This was Trump's first overt act to let Putin know that he was up for the job and had his back!!

It's not like we shouldn't do everything to improve relations between the two super powers, but Vladimir Putin has not shown the world that he is ready to be a good neighbor. In 2014, he annexed Crimea because he wanted direct access to the Black Sea for his navy. In July of 2019, he became a military ally with Syrian leader Assad who had been engaged in the genocide of his own people in order for Russia to have a Mediterranean seaport for his Russian navy. He continues to mock his Scandinavian neighbors with Russian fighter fly overs and violating their 12 mile international limit. He authorized cyber-attacks in the U.S. and European elections in 2016. Now that's the kind of power that Trump would like to have in the United States of America.

Well, there hasn't been a peep from his supporters nor the GOP since the Russians were in the Oval Room. This lack of objection emboldened him to continue with the dismantling of the inner workings of our government starting with the State Department. He refused to replace over fifty vacant posts in the State Department. Secretary of State, Rex Tillerson dodged every inquiry about not filling the vacancies which was a clear indication of Trump's intent to downsize the State Department period! Trump was not going to be needing more diplomats in the world that he was about to make over because they weren't needed and he was sure that he could oversee any diplomacy changes or diplomatic relationships that needed attention. Was he intentionally showing the world leaders and Putin that he was up to the job ahead?

Jared Kushner, President Donald Trump's son-in-law who was also one of Trump's senior advisers in the Trump administration had never held an upper level government position and he was now wanting to construct a private communications channel with the Kremlin. The Post reported that Kushner and Sergei Kislyak, the Russian ambassador to Washington, spoke on several occasions of coordinating a secret and secure communications channel between the Trump transition team and the Kremlin that even the NSA couldn't listen in on. Why would they need such a communication channel?

At the same time, a Reuter news report stated that Kushner had at least three previously undisclosed contacts with Russian Ambassador Kislyak during and after the 2016 presidential campaign. Those contacts included two phone calls between April and November 2016. Seven current and former U.S. officials confirmed the information with Reuters.

Jamie Gorelick, Kushner's attorney, told Reuters that her client couldn't recall any phone conversations with Kislyak between April and November of last year, "Mr. Kushner participated in thousands of calls in this time period. He has no recollection of the calls as described. Gorelick said, "We have asked (Reuters) for the dates of such alleged calls so we may look into it and respond, but we have not received such information yet,"

Where was the blowback when Trump began pulling us back from NATO under the guise of needing them to pay more for their military security. The entire world community knew that NATO was a thorn in Putin's side.

Trump's most important mission was to ensure the wealthy were given another tax cut (this would be the sixth since 1981) and the reason most wealthy people vote Republican. Second on his list was to repeal the Affordable Care Act (which didn't make sense because the ACA benefitted many Trump supporters).

I have to cut some slack here for those Americans forty years old and younger that had no Cold War or Dooms Day memories that us older Americans will never forget. Russia was hijacked by Bolsheviks thugs in 1917 after they murdered the Russian Tsar along with all of his family. They renamed Russia the USSR (Union of Soviet Socialist Republic) and they adopted a socialistic form of government called 'communism' wherein everyone was supposedly equal and all decisions were made by a Politburo which prevented any of them from ever being responsible when things went south; sort of like one of the old gangster movies in the 1940's when the crime bosses would get together to keep peace between each of their criminal families. Josef Stalin, Premiere in the 1930's suffered from acute paranoia and was said to have executed 6 million Russians that he thought could not be trusted because autocrats don't trust anyone.

The USSR ran out of money and came to an end in 1990. Mikhail Gorbachev was the leader at the time and he decided to let the people choose a leader going forward; big mistake! The U.S. under HW Bush chose to remain on the side line and let the Russian people take hold of their country knowing the Russians have had no history of taking such matters into their own hands; another big mistake! Missed opportunity for the U.S. and the GOP who was in power for they knew the Russians had no idea on how to form a democratic government.

So, it didn't happen! Boris Yeltsin, an independent politician and an active alcoholic, took hold of the struggling government. It didn't take long for another Russian named Vladimir Putin in St. Petersburg who was an ex-KGB agent returning from Romania to size up what was going on in Moscow and he came to Yeltsin's aid and capitulation. More importantly, the Russian people didn't blink an eye for this was the way the Russia they knew functioned. Putin took power after Yeltsin died of a heart attack and he has been in power ever since.

Vladimir Putin is a gangster. He surrounded himself with the leading oligarchs of Russia who filled his and their own personal coffers in order for them to stay rich, alive, in business, and in power. He pressured the Duma which is the Russian version of our Congress to vote and allow him to stay in power until 2036; Russia was better off under communism for Putin would have been executed long ago for stealing from the people, and for sure, someone like him would never have gone far in the Politburo scheme of things because he was all about himself, not his comrades.

In some ways though, it's worse than when the U.S. was in the Cold War, because back then the leader or Prime Minister of Russia as he was called answered to the Politburo; Putin answers to no man! This is a man who President Trump idolizes and wishes he could be for us in our country and have the same power as this man has in Russia. So, there you have it; simple but very dangerous; and we have people and leaders here in our country who have made it even more dangerous by their very ignorance and silence! I keep coming back to stupid is what stupid does, but I am of a mind that this is much more serious than that.

If damn near half of us do not have any idea what any of this may mean in terms of us having or not having dominion over our democracy, then we really are in tough straits. The founders were afraid we'd get wrapped up in our own worldly existence, not pay attention to what's going on here and abroad, let down our guard, not know our enemies or our friends, or worse, just not give a damn, and if this becomes the case, you don't have to be very bright to see what's in store for us. China, North Korea, Iran, Russia, and a few others are not by any means our friends or allies and they cannot wait to seize the moment when we are not paying attention. This is not a game for the light of heart, day dreamers, or fools and it is being used to separate us from each other. Remember, there are powerful behind the scene leaders, corporations, and political factions in America that make sure some of our leaders stay in power and decide on what will be used to take our eyes off the bouncing ball.

Chapter 5

Let's go back in time to our beginnings as a democracy. Were it not for the fifty four founding fathers and their spiritual moxie that drove them to put their entire fortunes on the line after signing the Declaration of Independence to fund this endeavor, there would not be a USA, and yet, just twenty years later after having won the war of independence, the southern colonies were going to walk out of the proceedings to ratify the Constitution in 1787 if the northern colonies did not approve of their use of slavery. It's important that you know what this was really all about because the same issue is in play today; money!

This meant, that the six southern colonies would only join the seven northern colonies to form a democratic republic if the constitution allowed them to continue to purchase black human beings kidnapped in Africa to use as their personal slaves, be allowed to trade these slaves, and use and abuse their slaves in order for them to achieve dominion over their personal and financial empires. This also meant that the everyday citizens in the south were in accord with all of this, for they understood the meaning of trickledown economics. To continue, this also meant that we as a nation did not have the moral compass to form a more perfect union coming out of the gate, and remember, it wasn't until four score and seven years later (75 Years) when the Civil War had been going on for a year that Abraham Lincoln did emancipate the slaves in September of 1862 against the advice of his team of Democrat rivals, but still not the result of a majority vote by the people! So, goodness as a virtue by the majority of this nation still did not prevail 75 years from the beginning our democracy or a 158 years ago! We need to ponder this fact.

Following the Revolutionary War, many of the early colonialists did not understand democracy nor did they think it could or would work, especially when some of them didn't even like each other let alone get along with each other. Others opined that this democracy business might work in Heaven if it really was the result of some divine intervention, but not here. Right from the git-go the founders and many of the state representatives feared this democracy business was going to be a treacherous slope, especially when they considered the skullduggery of some of the early revolutionary compatriots that ended up being traitors. This handicap is somewhat in play right now with some of the GOP leaders having more of an investment in Trump than they do to our democracy.

So, they were not very comfortable giving everyone the right to vote. They had lengthy discussions on who out of the populace would have the common sense, moral fiber, and mental acuity to evaluate the character of candidates for office and then cast their vote accordingly. It was not so much a case of intelligence as it was that they didn't believe everyone had the mindset to do the next right thing which they felt would be needed to grasp the great responsibility they were about to undertake in choosing those that would actually govern this new nation. There was no radio for officials to inform the populace as to the pros and cons of who should be allowed to vote and most of what the colonialists heard was hearsay. Remember too, the early colonists only knew what it was like to be subjects of a monarch; they did not know what it was going to mean for them to participate in having some responsibility for their own lives in a country that now belonged to them.

The representatives from each of the states grappled and debated over this until they decided only land owners (6% of the population) would be allowed to vote. This must have seemed unfair to some of those early patriots that fought in the war that didn't own land for they knew that if it wasn't for them this great experiment would not have happened. They evidently had some degree of humility, maturity, and spiritual acceptance that gave them the wherewithal to set their angst aside and become a part of this great experiment.

No matter, it also surely must've rubbed the non-land owners many of whom worked hard to provide for their families and just could not accumulate enough money to own a piece of land. Why did the founders think a landowner would have more of a moral compass and spiritual acuity than the non-land owners when it came to voting, especially when land parcels in the south and the north had been granted to trusted subjects by Kings James I, Charles I, Charles II, James II, Mary II, William III, Anne, George I, George II, and George III to ensure their faithfulness to the crown?

So, for 155 years, the above British monarchies were bestowing land grants to loyal British subjects to ensure allegiance to the crown because this was the only way Britain could manage their colonial empires all over the world. They were smart or at least wily enough to know they had to take care of those British expats that were somewhat indebted to the crown to ensure they would look after that which belonged to their king.

We come to 1787, and America no longer belongs to Great Britain or the king; it belongs to the citizens as a result of them having fought and won their freedom from the king, and yet, the founding fathers proclaim the only ones that deserve to vote will be those that are landowners! Did they not realize how corrupt or somewhat dangerous this was because most of the citizens knew most of these landowners like the Tories were still a bit closer to the crown than they were to this new idea called democracy. Talk about running with the hounds and sleeping with the foxes!

It took 81 years for the 14th Amendment to be ratified in 1868 which even then only gave the all-white males the right to vote. What was it that they understood or didn't understand in 1868 that gave way to them relaxing their control? Maybe Will Rogers hit the nail on the head when he said, "Anything important is never left to the vote of the people. We only get to vote on some man; we never get to vote on what he is to do."

Times and things were different. Folks back then were truly living on the edge. Those that ventured west got involved in the Indian wars and had little to no contact with mainstream America ever again.

So, what does all of this have to do with everyone having or not having a moral compass to cast his or her vote? Some of us today feel politicians would enlist the aid from the devil himself if it would help them win an election. Bingo! That's exactly why we need a moral compass! I say it matters a lot and without it we will not prevail! Those early patriots and we Americans ourselves are a patchwork quilt of personalities, dark traits, benevolence, malevolence, mental disorders, racism, xenophobia, kindness, meanness, lovingness, evilness, graciousness, spitefulness, humility, charitableness, and selfishness. It does us no good to try and take each other's inventory, for there is a little bit of the bad and good in all of us. However, it is not surprising how we behave towards each other, for it seems we do become more contemptuous of one another as we become more familiar with one another confirming the early adage of the patriots who believed familiarity breeds contempt. It's possible early Americans had one saving Grace that seems to be lacking amongst us today; they'd rather be content than right!

So, it seems to some degree or other, there was a sloping gradient to the moral compass of those early Americans that is still in play today that might best be described as different on different occasions for different generations. For sure, they were not a pampered lot as we are today. The world back then was competitive in a more tribal way whereas today we are competitive in a more individual, sophisticated, personal, or selfish way. Henri Nouwen was correct when he said, "To wait for moments or places where no pain exists, no separation is felt and where all human restlessness has turned into inner peace is waiting for a dream world."

They understood the saying "… striving to be good is the enemy of the best" and they were wise enough to know that demand, desire, or insistence for perfection would decrease their chances of obtaining a good or favorable result in the end; the Civil War probably began with the heavy drinkers in the taverns. We were and are today citizens of one of the most abundant nations on earth, but you would never know this by the way we believe enough is not enough which when talking about morality is gluttony in and of itself!

So, the founders opted to only let the folks who owned land vote and the rest including even those that fought in the war that gained their liberty, were not allowed to vote, and it didn't take long for the true colors of some of our trusted elder statesmen to come out as well.

The XYZ affair took place during the 2nd year of John Adam's presidency. Napoleon was in need of monies to support his insatiable appetite of dominating Europe and it didn't take long for him to target frigates on the high seas from the new country called the United States of America who were experiencing good economic times. In 1798, President Adams sent some emissaries to France to discuss a treaty that would include payment for the lost cargos and replacement of the 900 frigates that the French had sunk along with the return of all the U.S. sailors. The French government would not meet with the emissaries and they returned to the U.S..

Thomas Jefferson was the vice president and a member of the Democratic Republicans Party whereas John Adams was a Federalist. Adams won the vote for president; Jefferson was stunned and unable to believe that he been defeated. The 12th Amendment made it possible for the loser to become the vice president which Jefferson accepted which I think would have made his loss seem even more painful. Remember, Jefferson and Adams spent several years together trying to obtain aid from the French to fight our war with England. It was common knowledge around Paris that Jefferson was a womanizer or even worse because he had a wife back in America, but Adams never looked down on him and considered him to be his friend. So, it hurt Adams when Jefferson began undermining his policies with France and found an open ear with Alexander Hamilton to where they began in concert to get the populace in Philadelphia in an uproar against Adams because he wouldn't declare war against France. Some of this stems from when the French wanted President Washington to assist them in their war with England four years before and thank God Washington stood by the Neutrality Act.

So, it didn't take long for the issue to foment to where John Adams was an outsider in Philadelphia because of his continued discussions with the French ambassador trying to find an amiable solution with the French. Where did having or not having a moral compass come into play? I can say assuredly that we need always thank God for giving John Adams the wisdom, patience, and fortitude to stay the course. The XYZ emissaries returned to France and stayed the course through November 1799 to where Napoleon himself signed a treaty with America.

One can only imagine what would have happened to our fledgling nation had we gone to war with the French who would surely have given us a bashing at sea and mounted a ground invasion from their Louisiana Territory that bordered America to the west, and for sure, France would never have sold us the Louisiana Territory which means we would never have ventured west beyond the Mississippi!

So, what has all this to do with what is going on today; it should be clear! The troubles we don't handle well today will end up being settled more unfavorably tomorrow as this has always been the case when our compass drifts to a self-serving or immoral heading.

A case in point: my step-daughter came for a visit and my wife warned me, "She's an avid Trumper so you best don't want to be talking politics with her!" … "I'm not going to be talking politics with her or any family member." A few days later my step-daughter and I were sitting at the kitchen table at lunchtime waiting for some frozen pizza slices to heat up in the oven when one word led to another about something I said about Trump's behavior and she said, "I do not believe what the media says about Trump or anything else they say about him for that matter." … "What arc you basing that credibility on?" … "If I need to know about something, I turn on Fox News." … "What makes you think they're telling the truth?" … "I know they support Trump and they don't lie!" … "The facts prove otherwise though on 20,000 occasions that have been verified by every reputable news agency in the world." … "I don't believe any of them!" Before we knew it, our discussion was heating up faster than the pizza in the oven! I was so embarrassed that I was unable to abide by my intention not to get involved in any political discussions with her, and when I did, I lost it! My mouth got ahead of my brain to where I wasn't letting her speak her points which ended with both of us speaking over each other. Looking back, I was able to see that it was arrogant of me to assume that the moral truth would win out when in fact, the truth will only set you free when you know the truth; she did not care to know the truth and her truth could not be validated by her or anyone else! I lost control of my temper because she was not open to it, and it all happened in the blink of an eye!

····

The Civil War might not have happened if Susan B Anthony had been successful in winning the battle of suffrage for women to vote in the 1850's for I am sure they would have found a way to avoid the war. It was a terrible time for the suffragists and an even worse time for us as a nation. The South was tired of being demonized by the North for not giving up slavery and both sides were posturing themselves for war ... sound familiar? It wasn't all one sided either; Yankee Clipper ships funded by New York banks had been filling their holds with kidnapped black Africans for a hundred years to sell in the southern marketplaces. A discussion could not be had amongst either side at any level that didn't break out in a fight.

It took 73 years for the North and South to clash. The South said they went to war because of Yankee aggression and the North said they went to war because the South attacked Fort Sumpter. Looking back, it was clear that both sides had been on a collision course since 1787 when they couldn't settle the slavery matter before the signing of the Constitution. Goes to show what happens when we don't do the next right thing; the people get acrimonious, divisive, mean spirited, spiteful, dishonest, and hateful! Ring any bells? Don't forget the politicians that stoked the fever for war! The soldiers that died at Gettysburg were not losers or winners, but they were to some extent patsies who had been played by the powerful financiers of the North and plantation owners in the South and they were not going to let the profits from slavery that supported their economies and wealth slip quietly through their grasps; this was all about money!

We on this planet have had 137 major wars over the last 900 years which is a pretty sad epitaph for our species, but a good indicator of how we don't get along with each other, what can happen when we want to covet our neighbors goods or earn more money, how we are taken advantage of by our leaders, and worse, how we refuse to see our parts when we are having disagreements amongst ourselves which makes dealing with each other and nations an impossibility at best. In fact, we humans are a very clever species when it comes to covering up our dark sides and presenting a smiling persona that will deceive even the best psychiatrists.

As a nation, we Americans tend to congratulate ourselves on the great strides we have made in the area of diplomacy while at times we're busy undermining our neighbors. In a holier than thou pretense, the U.S. continues to remind the world every year since 1941 how the Japanese fleet conducted a sneak attack on our U.S. fleet at Pearl Harbor while the Japanese and U.S. delegates were discussing peace in Washington, DC., and yet, we too like the Japanese should bow our heads in shame whenever we are reminded of how our early all white leaders attempted to exterminate most of the Indian tribes across early America for defending their lands and fighting the white man as he drove west grabbing up all that land that really belonged to all the Indian nations who had lived here long before the white man had arrived in the first place! We whites not only did not honor one of the more than 500 treaties with the Indians, we then turned around and confined them forever to some of the worst and unlivable locations in our nation that we call reservations..

In 2002, I happened to be in Prattville, Alabama on business. While I was there, a friend and I went to see the first part of a two part movie called The Generals; it was a sellout. The first part was dedicated to the southern generals and the second part which was never completed would have been dedicated to the northern generals. About ten minutes into the movie, a scene opened that showed President Lincoln getting up from his desk in the White House to meet with Robert E. Lee. All 500 people in the theater stood up like they had been zapped by a Taser and started screaming and yelling expletives at the screen, "You sonofabitchin' bastard … no good whoremongering bastard … rotten no good yankee sonofabitch!" My friend and I were still seated and looking at each other in stark disbelief knowing they weren't directing this at Robert E. Lee. Never had I ever witnessed such an unexpected outburst of concerted hateful behavior such as this in all my travels. I sat there knowing to the innermost core of my being that for these people the clock had not moved one minute past the end of the Civil War.

And let us never, never forget the real consequences from John Wilkes Booth's dastardly deed when he assassinated Abraham Lincoln. There are no doubts from any of our historian's as to the great lengths Abraham Lincoln planned to go to reconstruct the South and repair our nation's wounds after the Civil War that heretofore have yet to be healed, like the folks in the movie theater. This quotation by Lincoln fell on deaf ears, "I am not bound to win, I am bound to be true. I am not bound to succeed, but I am bound to live up to the light I have."

This quotation has not stood the test for us today. There are few people to the left or right that may not want to talk about this, but since Trump arrived on the scene, this generation seems to have chosen to split or rupture the overall national fabric. Folks who have never identified with any of the so called far left or right positions in American politics, like the folks in the movie theater are front and center. Trump gave them all a picture of how this nation should look that pleased them; this is what they've been waiting for!

What some Americans saw as Trump's arrogance is seen by those that support Trump as audaciousness! Americans who have never felt like they were understood were now firing with all the same cylinders as Trump; they just couldn't foresee that they might be being played.

As described in Webster's dictionary, the meaning of the word arrogance in of itself suggests a darker side that I would rather not investigate, but it does intimate a lack of humility. It manifests itself with an attitude of superiority followed by an overbearing manner or presumptuous claims or assumptions followed by over twenty synonyms; bumptiousness, haughtiness, high horse, huffiness, imperiousness, loftiness, lordliness, pomposity, pretentious, superiority, toploftiness, and superciliousness followed by a short list of antonyms; humility, modesty, unassumingness, unpretentiousness, and some of these seem to fit Trump and his supporters to a tee. First known use of the word was in the 14th century which means it took mankind a long time to take a good look at themselves, and of course, as is the case with all character defects, we humans are always able to see them in others before we can see them in ourselves which means it is going to be difficult at best for this author because I planned on trying to present some of this with a kinder eye in order to keep everyone on the train.

What is different after four years of having Trump on the political scene is there are now 70 million plus people that feel they have found someone they can admire and trust. Many of them overlook or identify with Trump's narcissism, his telling of lies, his womanizing, gross exaggerations, and more than half are like my step-daughter who will not bear to hear the truth about him. Some have a distaste for Muslims, while others have no regard for people of color, and most of them do not see Trump as being a threat to our way of life and many would prefer his type of autocracy to what has been for them a very distasteful democracy, and most of them think our nation would undergo an improvement if he did serve another term.

This has never been about politics as much as it has been about that holier than thou attitude some of us get when we feel superior or lower than low to the next fellow which is negative pride. If we can get honest, we may can see how our lack of humility has prevented all of us from getting honest enough to see our parts in all of this. If we cannot get honest enough to see our parts in what's been taking place then we all will lose! The truth be known, most of us have been too preoccupied or afraid to seek the truth. The first stage of becoming a patsy is when we throw off the yokes of being honest with ourselves and start parroting what others are saying before we investigate, and when we do investigate, we fail because our shame is too painful or we have a pre-drawn conclusion in mind.

Some of this becoming a patsy business started with just wanting to fit in with the crowd that happened to have some different views that we adopted in favor of wanting to belong. Lemmings go over the cliff because they are following the one in front of them! So, again, if we're going to become our own person with a fair to middling compass, we must read reliable material that can be proven to be correct or incorrect. There are thousands of honest hard working reporters here and throughout the world every day trying to bring us factual information and up to date news that has not been adjusted or twisted to suit someone else's agenda. The news has been vetted and proven to be truthful which is the first casualty of many websites that have more of an investment in numbers, conspiracies, and radical beliefs.

Many Americans no longer read the written word. Folks that have not vetted the news and the sources of their news that they are passing on to others are guilty of passing on "fake news" which is making things worse for everyone. People that use unreliable sources that are steered to so called crafted websites that correlate with the individual's profile could be getting news that is slanted, tampered with, or made to please the user. So, sophistication itself may have become the determining factor of what is or isn't truthful and if that doesn't scare you, what will?

There is overwhelming proof that Trump publicly made over 22,000 false statements. If some of his followers continue to believe otherwise and they have not asked themselves "What's with all the lying?" then they become part of the problem. Why would they not wonder why he's been telling all these lies? If I can learn to listen like I didn't do with my step-daughter, and be extra sure that I understand what she is saying, then and only then can I be sure that I as well am playing with a full deck; otherwise we will be no earthly good for each other. It's one thing to have an opinion or mindset, it's something else when we try and convince others that we are right if we are not open to the truth, especially a truth that can be confirmed. This is arrogance at its worse that sets us all up to be played and becoming patsies! I'll bet your kids even know better!

As I see it, We the People and that means you and I, are only here by the Grace of God as were those courageous pilgrims that landed at Plymouth in 1620; or those courageous patriots that chose to bear arms against their unjust king; or encouraged the fifty four founding fathers to lay their entire fortunes on the line after signing the Declaration of Independence. Otherwise this great experiment would never have taken place and that in and of itself would have been the greatest tragedy. These people were individuals just like you and I.

So, to what end were the founders thinking when they conceived this great idea called democracy? How did they think we were going to operate as a people within the framework of this Constitution which some thought was nothing more than a gentlemen's agreement? Some of them didn't even like one another, some of the Tories lamented their loss of a king hoping one day they would all return to the kingdom. How did the founders envision everyone would be willing to work together to form a more perfect union?

For starters, they weren't a sophisticated lot like most us are today and they worked long hours by the sweat of their brows to eke out a meager economical existence fraught with hardships, diseases, and extreme weather conditions. They did however believe a penny saved was a penny earned which is something America gave up on years ago in favor of a credit card when we were seduced into believing instant gratification was going to save their day. For the most part, the colonialists were not so religiously minded as they were spiritually fit in ways that many of us don't know about today which was evident by their slogan, 'In God We Trust' that they lived by and stamped on all their coins and currency.

It certainly does seem they were a bit naïve when you consider there were no details on how they were going to remedy some of the violations or transgressions to the Constitution. For instance, they wrote that the president could be impeached by Congress for high crimes and misdemeanors, and yet, they didn't bother to list some of the crimes or discuss what would happen when the President and the Senate were of the same political faction making it unlikely they would condemn one of their own. There have been five impeachments and not once has the Senate condemned one of their own. And what would happen if the impeached president would not go quietly, and if he didn't, who was going to make him leave. Then of course, there have been those elected leaders over the last 200 years that were in step with these loose ends which led to many of us to becoming played and not knowing it.

Surely, they understood the human condition from the traitors and scalawags that damn near prevented them from winning the Revolutionary War, so again, why were they so vague? There were no democratic republics for them to copy and most monarchies or autocracies that were toppled almost always returned much the same or worse. So, I believe they didn't want to get bogged down or overburdened with rules and explicit details lest they lose momentum and pronounce this democratic experiment too cumbersome, too difficult, and dead on arrival. I'm also sure there were some folks that would have preferred their states became a sovereign nation and not have to worry about all these rules that were being made so that all the states could get along as one. I also would surmise that expediency was most important for we all know what happens when you dilly-dally. The founders worked long hours every week in 1787 to get the Constitution completed before the end of the year. They did not spend time peeking behind the human veil to see if it was reasonable to assume the Supreme Court Justices were going to be able to perform their duty interpreting the written words of the Constitution vs the political interpretation wanted by the party that was in power that made them a justice. But isn't that what they all must've been thinking when they finished and proclaimed, "We'll just have to figure this out on the run and that means 'Us'.

When I turn the calendar back to the time when the founders were deliberating on who should have the right to vote for the first congressmen, senators, and president, I come to the same conclusion because they knew it was going to be easier to add voters than it was to remove some voters. Secondly, they didn't want the first election to have any mistakes. So, it maybe was not so much a case of keeping different folks from voting as much as it was getting it as close to right coming out of the gate.

Everyone might not have liked each other, but I believe they did have each other's backs from the time they got off the boat at Plymouth Rock and Jamestown for they knew they would not survive the constant hardships and friction with the British authorities which brings me to a very important part of this book. I believe from the git-go that there were constant political forces in play most of which were created by the British to keep the colonialists off balance when it came to taking sides against the British Crown and the British rule of law. There were the colonial collaborators that were always sucking up to the British authority to ensure they would receive some perks when the going got tough; it's what some of us humans do. Some of our politicians behave this way today. So, with that in mind, I think the people found themselves in somewhat of a damned if we do and damned if we don't situation which is exactly how the British wanted it to be. They had to conceal their discontent, not talk to one another about irritations, not chat with people they didn't trust, refrain from squabbling in public over political issues and political figures so as to ensure they would appear to have become the patsies the British intended them to be! Ring any bells!

So, back to the group of Russians that were clandestinely invited into our Oval Room in May of 2017 by the newly elected Trump who himself was still under investigation after 17 different intelligence agencies from around the world corroborated that he and some of his campaign managers did in fact have ongoing meetings and collaborate with high level Russians right up to election day which in of itself is illegal because our laws prohibit using foreign state influences during a campaign, and yet, all his supporters and nearly every GOP politician in Washington turned a blind eye and deaf ear to it all while Trump proclaimed, "I won ... the rest is fakes news ... get over it!"

Chapter 6

Since the beginning of civilization, we humans have had a tendency to exaggerate the truth when telling a story which is considered hyperbole. It can also be used to hold the attention of the listener and usually has no malevolent intent. The intelligence agencies around the world go a step beyond hyperbole when they seed untruths in order to create misdirection in order to lead their adversaries down a yellow brick road.

Then there is intentional disinformation that when used as a constant in your own homeland can undermine the general public's faith in each other and their government which is what took place when Hitler and Mussolini were coming to power; this is called propaganda or fascism. Eventually, the citizens don't know who or what to believe and end up disregarding all the information being given them, some of which may be the truth. The purpose of this type of disinformation is to keep the public off balance so that they cannot discern what is real or unreal with respect to what their leaders are actually up to until it's too late which was the case with Germany and Italy; the public woke up one morning and Hitler and Mussolini were their leaders for life. Remember, the entire world was in a depression and this along with disinformation and outright lies can be used to gain control of any nation that lets down their guard and almost always ends with autocratic or dictatorial control.

The motto for fascists is: Believe, obey, fight. The motto for democracy is Life, Liberty, and the pursuit of Happiness ... the motto for our leaders and military is supposed to be Duty, Honor, and Country. A six year old on tv was asked what he thought honor meant and he said, "If you do something and you feel ashamed you haven't acted with honor" ... out of the mouth of babes we get the right answer.

There have always been mean spirited rulers; take the Etruscans that lived in what is now Italy in 900 bc. They became what we know were the Romans in 400 bc. They were a very intelligent people, but they were also mean-spirited. They built coliseums and arenas for combat sports using gladiators that fought to the death to amuse the citizens. Right about the same period, the Greeks landed in what is now Loci, Italy and they built amphitheaters that used culture and plays to entertain their people. Two completely different worlds on the same planet; one vicious and one dedicated to the humanities.

So, never in the course of our nation's history has any president sowed so many untruths, over 22,000 at this writing, and yet his supporters ask, "What's this got to do with us ... it's just the way he is ... lighten up!" Have you all noticed how we were all aghast when the lies began, but not anymore. We now have come to take the lies in stride which is exactly how this type of disinformation is supposed to work and exactly how it worked in 1933. Have you noticed how Trump did not get upset when he was called out by a reporter for speaking a previous lie; he just changed the subject and moved on to another topic which is exactly what you're supposed to do if you have been trained or have an autocratic or fascist mindset. He also may be more of a reader than we give him credit for.

Trump admires autocrats to a fault which is probably why he started taking trips to Russia in 1987 before the USSR came to an end. He somehow cultivated a relationship with folks in the Kremlin that later may have led him to Vladimir Putin who was a once upon a time summa cum laude ex-KGB agent and maybe Donald Trump's mentor as well. The world will never forget when Trump and Putin came out of their two hour long meeting to meet with the press in Helsinki; Putin looked like the master and Trump looked like the pupil who had just been given his marching orders. Funny thing about leaders who are running with the foxes and sleeping with the hounds, they must always have the wherewithal to know which one they're supposed to be at all times; Putin absolutely knew who he was supposed to be that day and how he should behave; Trump wasn't that good at this then, but he's getting there!

Putin as an ex-KGB officer is a master at disinformation and guile which has made his relationship with Trump suspicious at best. Putin yearns for Russia to return to those days when they were the USSR.

This might be a good place to inform those who were not paying attention in their history classes how Hitler and Putin came into power.

Hitler hated communism when he was coming into power in 1930, and he knew he would attack Russia if and when he had the opportunity, but until then, Hitler signed a non-aggression pact with Stalin who was the leader of Russia in August of 1939. Germany failed in their attempt to crush England after three months of bombings during the Battle of Britain in 1940 and Hitler turned at once to invading Russia which was his biggest mistake. FDR who was the president of the U.S. authorized military assistance for the Russians and began shipping millions of tons of war materials to Murmansk, Russia which may have been his first major mistake. Some of FDR's advisers considered the Russian communists as much of a threat to world peace as Germany and were not so keen on giving Russia military aid. They knew the U.S. would soon be drawn into the war and thought it wiser to let Russia and suffer heavy mutual military losses. U.S. strategic bombers would be laying waste to every German city which would compel Germany to agree to unconditional surrender. Communist Russia would lie in economic ruin and would not have a role part in the post war rebuilding of the rest of Europe going forward.

That's not what happened! The German invasion failed and Russia finally got the upper hand having received millions of tons of war supplies from the U.S. They recaptured all the eastern European territories that Germany had captured. As the war was coming to a close, a seven day meeting took place in February 1945 at Yalta between FDR, Churchill, and Stalin wherein FDR who should not have gone to this meeting because he was very seriously ill, announced to the group that the U.S. was in favor of giving Russia custodial responsibility over all the countries that they had won back from the Germans. This was beyond incomprehensible! Our allies and our own military leaders were dumbfounded. It literally sentenced most of the people of Europe who were the victims of the war to a life under the boot of communism along with abject poverty for the next 36 years. This was thought to be beyond being the cruelest mistake made by anyone during WW II and it was done by our president, FDR! But could it be that FDR thought this was going to be the best way of securing peace throughout Europe when the war was over?

The economy in Russia imploded in 1989 bringing the USSR to its end. To rub salt into our wounds, Russia has denied to this very day that they ever received any war materials from the U.S.

Thirty-seven year old Putin returned from Romania in 1990 to find Russia which had been one of the most powerful countries on earth reduced to a 4th rate power. He was hired as deputy mayor of St. Petersburg and began using his position to shake down international carpetbaggers wanting to do business in what everyone thought was going to be a free Russia. Then he saw his moment for fame in Moscow when Yeltsin, a floundering alcoholic was unable to secure power and set Russia back on its feet. Yeltsin on his death bed admitted bringing Putin into his circle was a betrayal to the Russian people ... he realized too late that Putin only wanted to return Russia back to the days of the USSR for himself.

.....

Trump does not agree with citizens having a right to protest against him, his administration, local government or law enforcement even though to protest in our nation is a time honored practice of speaking out against perceived injustices, and more so, is a form of assembly protected by our Constitution. He ordered Chad Wolf, acting DHS Secretary to send uniformed military contractors in full battle gear without any unit insignias to Portland to put down the unrest; not good!. Hitler used the brown shirts to put down riots that his own squads had created. Trump's base couldn't wait to send some of their gun toting militia into the streets as well and the result was Portland went from protesting to a full scale riot. This is exactly what the autocratic script is supposed to look like; first there's civil unrest and then the wannabe autocrat will use this unrest as an excuse to send in the riot squads to beat them back to appear as if he has saved everyone.

American intelligence officials have released information that a Russian military intelligence unit was secretly paying bounties to the Taliban militants for killing coalition forces and American troops in Afghanistan. President Trump was livid when the press released this editorial and he avoided mentioning the issue to a fault; mum was the word in the GOP Senate as well. Why was there not a peep from the GOP Senate or Trump supporters on this one? This was the most un-American an American could be! Who are these people? If any American had a part in this they should be tried for treason.

Trump made a major blunder when one of his staff told a reporter that he overheard the president say he was not going to ride 35 miles to Aisne-Marne Cemetery in the rain when they were in France on Memorial Day to pay tribute to the fallen U. S. Marines that were buried there and then referred to them as 'losers and suckers'. I do not believe this was a misstatement as much as it was him putting another feeler out to the netherworld to see how far he could go before he was dragged out of the WH and he got his answer; he didn't even come close to having to wash his mouth out with soap and his so called base of patriots are not interested in such matters.

Qanon is a media disinformation outfit that the FBI has had their eye on since they began appearing at the Trump rallies in 2018. President Trump has been overly fond of them which doesn't surprise anyone, especially the FBI and CIA who I believe are the last ramparts of our Republic.

The FBI called the Qanon a bunch of conspiracy theory-driven domestic extremists that very likely will emerge, spread, and evolve in the modern disinformation marketplace, occasionally driving both groups and individual extremists to carry out criminal or violent acts, like the 14 extremists from the Wolverine Watchmen Group that were just arrested in Michigan for plotting to kidnap the Governor. Are you are all still with me?

What's upsetting about sects like this is they tend to think they're the ones putting a spin on disinformation when it's them that the dark powers to be are going to use and blame for the misinformation, and use as a scapegoat. Dangerous stuff this seeding of autocracy business, especially for the citizens who haven't a clue of who is doing what to who, but for sure they will be the patsies as will always be the case when government leaders are flirting with autocracy. Most Europeans didn't see any of this coming when they were bungling their way into fascism and autocracies before World War II.

Election Day is 12 days away. The Russians, Chinese, North Koreans, and Iranians are busy trying to hack into our voting precincts and waging cyber warfare against our election process. Trump didn't have much to say about this subject as well when a reporter queried him for a comment.

The Constitution allows each sovereign state to decide how their citizens will cast their votes. This didn't set well with Trump because he felt this would serve the Democrats more than the GOP voters which was his way of suggesting this election would be a fraud if he lost the election. Has anyone noticed how he never thought the 2016 election was a fraud?

President Trump used his lawyers to try and prevent mail-in ballots from being counted 3 days after Election Day. The Pennsylvania courts rejected this petition which Trump hoped they would do thinking this would open the door for him to petition the Supreme Court with his three newly appointed justices. It would be impossible for a screen writer in Hollywood to try and bring such a plot like this to a successful conclusion!

It also goes to show what can happen when we send scalawags and opportunists to Washington DC to enact laws and manage our nation that ends up with them creating a world that suits them, but not us. All that is happening in Washington DC is a direct reflection on <u>our</u> lack of discernment and involvement in taking the time to investigate the characters of these so called trusted servants, candidates, and officials long before we get to the ballot box. We must learn to set aside our political investments on each candidate until we were absolutely sure they have the character and spiritual mettle to become a trusted servant which brings you and I back to the same issue that continues to thread its way through this book, our moral acuity.

The founders were worried sick about this very issue and we should be worried about it as well today. How would it be possible for a voter with little to no moral capacity or fortitude to advocate and ensure that they have used due diligence to ensure their likely candidate has the moral character and fiber to lead our nation going forward? Almost never! Or worse, who would a white supremist, anarchist, racist, extremist, or home grown terrorist nominate to represent them in a democratic nation?

So then, democracy really starts with We the People, not with some of the disinformation creators or miscreants running for office! We will always be the problem if we don't have the moral fortitude with which to vet the truth and select our leaders; just look at how Lindsay Graham has immorally navigated his way through the morass created by Trump over the last four years; he's an expert at running with the hounds and sleeping with the foxes.

Chapter 7

We've all been to a carnival or fair where a hawker invites a passerby to point to one of the three shells on the table that they thought the pea was under after the hawker had shuffled them every which way around the table. As it turns out, this is exactly what happened to the two major political parties.

The landscape for American politics in the first half of the 1800's was made up of the Democratic-Republican Party, the Whigs, the Federalists, and the Know-Nothing Party. During this period, slavery was the main issue throughout the nation leaving most Americans in two opposing groups; those for or against slavery.

In 1824, the Democrats joined with the more conservative elements of the Republican Party resulting in the Democrat-Republican Party. The now standalone Republican Party came onto the scene in 1855 with its members from the former Whigs and some liberals from the Democratic-Republic party in the North. The Democrats, especially in the South, became the primary haven of the pro-slavery elements of society and the Republicans became the party of the abolitionists.

The Democrats served the industrialists, plantation owners and professional classes; the Republicans served the farmers and industrial workers. The Democrats were more dedicated to foreign policy and the Republicans paid more attention to the homeland issues like building up the infra-structure and creating national parks. Evangelicals, Christians, and Southern Baptists were most likely to vote for a Democrat, while Christians in general like the Methodists, voted Republican. The Democratic Republican party served the conservatives in the South and the standalone Republican Party served the liberal minded in the North. Remember this point!

So, as one can see, before the Civil War, the Democrats were the conservatives and the Republicans were the liberals. Remember this as well! So how exactly did the two parties switch polarity? Immigrants! Immigrants began arriving towards the middle of the 19th century. The South having lost the Civil War in 1865 left the Democratic Party floundering and the Republicans were not welcomed in the South leaving them to fill the seats of power in Washington DC for most of the elections for the next fifty years which left an economic and political vacuum in the South.

Irish Catholics started coming to America in droves which filled the quotas for Tammany Hall, a New York city political organization founded in 1786 which also added the needed votes for the Republican Party. By the turn into the 20th century, industrialists who had long been connected with the Democrats now realized that the Democrats were the party that served labor and they began to switch back to the Republican Party.

One of the great fears that the American middle class always had concerning immigration is the competition provided by cheap labor, and it was a valid concern. The immigrants were known to be hard workers and usually a recession followed each wave of immigrants for a brief period until the new immigrants settled into America. But immigrant labor also had a tendency to cost more as time went on. Immigrants came to America for economic opportunity, but they also came for political and religious freedom which prompted many of them to get into the political mix and become active. The so called liberal Democrats thought they were getting easy votes, but what they ended up with was a huge cadre of voters seeking higher wages and better working conditions; and they were not passive! By the early 1900's, immigrant labor had mushroomed. Conservative Democrats in the south were not greatly affected by these developments, however, large numbers of wealthy industrialists and middle class business owners in the North began defecting to the Republican Party in order to protect their wealth.

The Republican Party, in the meantime, watched with growing concern as their long time hold on the federal government began to slip. They represented the wealthy class and the financial markets, but they lacked the number of voters needed to win at the polls. The South still regarded the Republicans as the power that destroyed the South in the Civil War and was not yet heading in their direction.

The Great Depression removed the Republican Party from every level of power across the land leaving Franklin D. Roosevelt and the Democrats in full control of the government for the next twelve years. It would take a generation for the Republicans to recover. By the end of the Roosevelt era, American labor and the unions had won their battle for higher wages and working conditions. Democrats began turning their attention to civil rights for blacks in the South which caused many of their voters in the North to flee to the Republicans which lets us see early on that racialism played a significant role in politics back then as well.

So, there you have it. The two major parties did a complete flip-flop landing on their feet supporting the opposite group of people they started with and leaving each party with a moniker that really belonged to the other in the past but none the less, proved to be what each party really stood for now. The so called liberal Democrats did prove to be the conservatives when it came to fiscal management and paying down the debt, whereas the so called conservative Republicans were fast becoming the liberals for exceeding their budgets, over spending for the military complex and liberally allowing tax cuts that benefitted the wealthy with money that we didn't have that increased the debt.

The Democrats originally were the party for the industrialists, plantation owners, and professional classes; the Republicans were for the farmers and factory workers. For the last 100 years right up to now, the Democratic Party has supported what is called the middleclass and labor, the Republicans support corporations, the military industrial complex, professional classes, and farmers. The Republicans continue to remain more focused on domestic issues. Until Roe vs Wade, Evangelical and independent Christians, notably Southern Baptists, generally voted Democratic, while more traditional Christians, notably Methodists, tended to vote Republican. The Democratic stronghold was the conservative South, while the Republican stronghold was the liberal North. That all switched as well!

There was a time when Americans voted, accepted the outcome, and got on with their lives. Not anymore! The politicians, TV news networks, and smart phone media tries to keep everyone in a state of political flux which may be good for the politicians but not good for us. Trump spent

$800 million during the last month of his campaign on television ads and you do not have to be smart to know how this was appreciated by the media!

So, where does the average middle-class voter fit in all of this. Rather than both parties having a similar vision for all of America going forward, we now have two parties with absolutely no common policies because they each have a different flock of voters with different wants and a different vision of what America should look like and therein lies the confusion and rub for the present day average American voter, and by average American, I mean you and me not them and us.

Will Rogers may have said it best, "Democrats never agree on anything, that's why they're Democrats. If they agreed with each other, they'd be Republicans."

The first question you must ask yourself is which party benefits who in America otherwise you will surely be played and end up a patsy; you cannot be what you cannot see! As explained above, the Republican Party went from the party that freed the slaves and being demonized by the South to the party that welcomed all the Southerners who now wanted to save the South from the blacks that used to be the slaves. More importantly, this one issue has become the banner issue for most white Americans across the country who are not comfortable with the black population out numbering the whites in their communities to where they now can see their white ethnicity becoming extinct! This one issue has become the claxon for whites to come together and create a buffer to save their white heritage for their future generations. Easier said than done! All they have to do is stop being so selfish and start having more babies; 1.3 babies per white family vs three to four for families of color tells it all. But still, if you do have issues with people of color, then the Republican Party may be the party for you, however, this too is sure to change someday as well.

If you are a person of color that wants representation in Washington DC, then the Democratic Party will welcome you with open arms until such time of course when a different status quo becomes an irritant and then we're all back to square one. I keep coming back to the three or four party system as the only solution for everyone to feel included and have equal representation, especially since the people of color will soon outnumber the white people. Maybe it's time for the people of color to create a new party and began sending leaders to Washington DC which will allow the art of compromise to begin anew!

••••

Lets not forget! There were 17.4 million manufacturing jobs in the U.S. when GW Bush took office and 11.5 million when he left. 70 thousand businesses closed up under GW Bush and re-opened overseas using high corporate taxes as the reason they left. Hogwash! They wanted to increase their overall margins tenfold and the only way they could do that was with cheap labor. American workers were left high and dry long before the Great Recession hit. Again, when you're looking to hitch your wagon to a major political party, you need to do your homework to see which one is looking out for your best interests. This global economy idea may fit well with the GOP, but not the average American worker. There are some advanced thinking economists that believe automation is going to wreak havoc on the middle class workers to where the government will be paying each of them $1500 a month to do nothing! Talk about people feeling miserable because they are no longer needed!

The Great Recession hit just before the 2008 national election. This was a snapshot in time that let you see exactly who the Republican Party was looking out for when the bubble burst and it wasn't the average person of color or white American in the street. No, it was those Americans who had serious money in the stock market. The very first thing the Bush Administration did was create the $475 billion TARP bailout (Troubled Asset Relief Program) which reimbursed all these wealthy folks who were about to lose most of their investment monies when the investment banking companies were going belly up on Wall Street. How's that for a government having the backs of a select few to keep them from taking a hit in the investment market? I think the founding fathers would have had plenty to say about this!

Obama granted loans to the automobile factories after the financial crisis began to ensure the auto companies and their suppliers could keep their employees on the jobs in the Mid-Western states of Ohio, Indiana, Michigan, and Wisconsin. The voters from these states didn't return the favor by showing up to vote in the 2010 midterm and this stripped the legislative power from the Democrats leaving Obama unable to achieve his agenda. It's this fickleness of the Democrat voters that makes no rhyme or reason when it comes to turning your back on the party that did have your back which puts the blame squarely with the Democrat voters; they have failed on a large scale to show up for midterm elections. This allows all that was gained in a national election to be set aside and returned to square one which brings us back to what the founders were concerned with when it came to giving everyone the right to vote vs only allowing those to vote who are sensible, mature, and responsible. In other words, there's a lot of irresponsible and fickle Democrats that don't show up to vote that maybe should not have the right to vote or should be fined if they don't vote because it is their obligation to vote!

With all of the above in mind, if you are an everyday working stiff like most Americans are, why in God's name would you ever vote for a GOP candidate if they're never, ever going to have your back like they do for their wealthy benefactors? You would be a patsy for sure and justifiably so! Ever asked yourself why patsies don't find it necessary to get involved with the details until it's too late?

Here's another great example of stupid is what stupid does! Why would you as a student from the middle class vote for a GOP candidate that supports students paying high student loan interest rates vs a Democrat that wants you to have a free basic college education? The 20 top GDP nations and even Bolivia have free tuition for all college students! Can you imagine the outstanding brain power, manufacturing power, and buying power that our country would have if every person had a basic college degree? The million dollar question is, why isn't the Republican Party in favor of everyone having access to a free basic college education? They'll tell you they're being conservative and that's hogwash. It's competition! Republicans are selfish and don't want competition for their offspring!

I believe the GOP fear of competition will be their undoing. If you look back to the beginning of our nation you will see that there was a spiritual truth in play from the beginning that clearly demonstrated, 'We will not be able to keep what we have unless we are willing to give it all away!' Think about it! How else did we accomplish all that has been done? I submit that if each one us in main stream America had not been given a leg up or a break, we as a nation would never have been able to succeed to where we became the light for the free world which has made us better off for it as well; it was that way for me! It's God's way of saying to each of us, 'Do unto each other that which you would hope would be done unto you!' Stinginess and competition are killers and have no place in this world let alone a democratic society! So, if we each remember to keep giving it away without any strings attached then we all will be the richer for it.

Let's take a closer look at the benefits of a four party system, I've been wondering why someone or some group like the Millennials hasn't stepped up, taken hold, and re-organized the Independent Party that was established in 1967. For all intents and purposes, the Independents just sit on the fence and never take an overt political position on any issue which means they don't have any skin in the game. They pick and choose candidates from the other two parties without any risk which allows the other two parties to duke it out and we end up getting nowhere. A fully active three or four party system wherein all the parties elect leaders would eliminate a great deal of the political rancor and force the leaders that are sent to Washington DC to work and compromise with another which really hasn't been the case for the last 234 years. No longer would one party be in charge.

155 million Americans voted in the 2020 election out of 239 million registered voters. The first question one must ask is who are those 84 million voters that didn't show up to vote. 53 million of the 84 million registered voters think things will continue as they are now regardless if they vote. So, 155 million voters did show up and vote which is the highest number of people to ever vote in a national election. There are four political parties in the UK, four political parties in Germany, four political parties in Japan, and four political parties in Brazil. Each of these four countries have 66 million, 82 million, 126 million, and 212 million respectively. The population of the U.S. is 330 million people, and yet we have three parties of which only two are fully active parties that send 98% of all the representatives and senators to the Capitol; the third party sends only a few elected leaders to Washington and the voters end up voting for candidates from the other two parties. No wonder we are having problems governing our country when 84 million don't even show up to vote which is more voters than the UK has and as many voters as there are in Germany. The 84 million voters didn't vote because they don't feel they are represented by any of the three parties. If they formed a 4th party they could possibly attract 40 million voters.

This also means that people of color and those from every economic level across the country would be sought after by four parties represented in Washington DC and every state capitol throughout the land and this too is what the founders had hoped our government would look like someday. Remember, we as a country are only 234 years old and we have a lot to learn if we truly want to be happy and get along with one another and the rest of the world.

More importantly, a four party system might prevent us from unraveling into a tragedy that no one will be happy with; we've already done that once and we surely do not want to go there again. There is no way this is going to work if we all don't come together; black, white, brown, and yellow and get along with all of our indifferences that can only be solved when we all get involved and make a difference. We need always be open to each other's points of views, improve our listening and reading skills, and see each other as fellow travelers in the universe; we're not on some self-serving back road or alley way that lead us to nowhere.

An elected official needing support for a bill is going to have to cross over three aisles to the members of the other three parties if he or she needs support for a bill or a cause and visa-versa. As it is now, the party that has control of Congress or the Senate can stonewall the other party and there's not a damn thing that they can do about it. Not so with a fully active three or four party system for they will all have to conduct themselves with mutual respect and honesty if they ever hope to succeed in getting fifty percent of the Senate or Congress behind a bill or stopping a motion. And lastly, in a four party system there will be many times when two or three of the four parties will need to keep the other party in check when it is overstepping or misusing its power. In the meantime, the Democrats and Republicans continue playing their good cop bad cop routine which is never ever going to be good representation for all the people. It's obvious for everyone to see the difference between a two legged stool and a three or four legged stool.

I have always faulted the Democrats for never blowing their horn and letting the world really know how they've been most fiscally conservative when it came to paying down the accumulated debt from WW II, the Cold War, the Korean War, and the Vietnam War that totaled $15.8 trillion. Using a 72% tax rate on the wealthy, the debt had been paid down to $985 billion. Ronald Reagan came on the scene and he immediately gave two tax cuts to the wealthy that forced him to begin borrowing money for the revenue shortfall which put the debt back up to $2.8 trillion when he left office. Most countries use a marginalized tax that kicks in around 60% of the $100,000 earnings to insure a level playing field. The GOP on the other hand protects the wealthy from paying higher taxes period. Some wealthy Americans only paid an 8.5 % adjusted tax in 2019 leaving the rest of the tax payers to pay the revenue needed for the annual budget which is not enough which results in the need to borrow huge sums of money to run the country! The GOP is protecting 3% of the people in our country from paying their fair share and if there's not enough revenue to meet the budget then they'll borrow the money! To make matters worse, the wealthy donate some of these tax savings to PAC funds that will be used to keep the Republican Party in power. I would love to hear what any one of our founders might have thought about this program. They might just say the rest of us are a bunch of jackasses and need to figure it out and change it! A fully active four party system would do that!

Keep in mind and never forget, there are those in this world that oppose our way of life and there are those whose main purpose is to drive a wedge between each of us when we do not see eye to eye, for that's when we become putty in the hands of those who do not have our true interests at heart. Ring any bells?

Every generation in this nation has had their difficulties and there are times when politicians will use these times to their selfish advantage which will not solve our problems! We need to hold them accountable and not become so invested or embroiled in our politics, religions, or ethnicities that we take our eyes off the bouncing ball to where we each become no earthly good!

I believe some of the ideas and intentions Donald Trump had when he was running for president might may have worked and may have happened if he wasn't so distrustful. Not having trust means he was going to have to do everything himself and therein lies his failure. A president's main job is to hire the best people there are and give them every bit of support and assistance they will need to succeed. Much of what goes on in the international world is overseen by our diplomats in the State Department which he didn't trust which in of itself was self-defeating at best when it came to having success with trade, NATO, and nuclear disarmament treaties, and of course, nothing of any meaningful diplomatic value was accomplished during Trump's presidency.

I feel the best when I pause and remember all the young men and women of our great nation who came together the day after Pearl Harbor was attacked on December the 7th, 1941. Regardless of their color, politics, sex, and ethnicities. Millions from the farms, industrial cities, north, and south showed up to enlist at their local recruiters the first thing on the morning of December 8th! They found themselves fighting alongside other fellow Americans that they would never have met let alone trusted their lives to in what was the greatest of all wars. This is who we were and should still be today, and yet, this did not happen after 9/11 for only several thousand showed up the next day to join the service; not millions! Why! Again, it's what Abraham Lincoln meant when he gave the Gettysburg Address, **"It is for us the living, rather, to be dedicated here to the unfinished work which they who fought here have thus far so nobly advanced."** He meant all of **'Us'**!

I'm reminded of what happened in the 1952 Election when President Eisenhower who was running for president promised us he'd have 'our boys' home by Christmas from the Korean War; didn't happen and that war ended two years later in a stalemated truce that exists to this very day that left many back then feeling a lot less proud to have gone to war and come home not winning! Never should a politician, and especially an outstanding general like Eisenhower who led armed forces to victory in WW II make a promise to the voters he couldn't keep in order to win an election. And let's not forget, few politicians have ever had any skin in any of our wars. They're big on getting us into wars and short on duty, honor, country when it comes to finishing them like we did in World war II and Desert Storm. Most importantly, we should never get into a war without the will of the people to win! Never! Ever!

That's where we the people come in and if we don't have the spiritual moxie to elect the best men and women to do the job, then more of us are going to end up being played.

Politicians have a way of running with the foxes one week and sleeping with hounds the next. Some of that is nothing more than posturing so as to let their constituents think they're really working hard for them and their causes. I guess that's ok if you don't have any integrity and don't want to act like adults, but most times it reeks of arrogance when they're the ones that should be honest, fair minded, and have a moral compass. They all swore an oath to protect the Constitution but few actually do it. Maybe this is an 'Aha' moment! And if it is, it can only happen if the people that are voting have spiritual principles and use them to select their leaders in the voting booth.

Ever wonder why so many Americans are having a love affair with guns? This too is one of the down sides of doing away with the draft. Most combat soldiers come home from the war not caring if they ever see a gun again whereas some of the wannabee soldiers that attend paint ball assault meets and live at the shooting ranges are living in a dark combat dream world. Just look at the billions of dollars that kids can win on the world circuit digital war game meets; not healthy and for some it develops into an addiction accompanied with severe mental health issues.

Chapter 8

I took a break from writing to go out front and get the morning paper and met a man walking his dog, "Good morning" … "Good morning to you sir" … "You watch the debate last night?" … "I did. Not a pretty picture" … "Surely didn't resemble the first debate 60 years ago" … "No, it didn't" He was an elderly man like myself and I continued, "I believe we're all being played and if there's one thing I hate, it's being played!" … "Same here, no one likes being played, but what can we do about it, it's been going on too long now" … "I guess just recognizing it gets us off point. I get mad every time I see the amount of our national debt which I believe is the main part of this whole charade!"

The dog was pulling on the leash wanting to move to the next spot down the street when the man responded, "President Clinton was the last president to have a balanced budget" … "That's right! He left office $250 billion under budget! It all started with President Reagan when he ran rough shod over everything. He wasn't in office a few days when he repealed the funding for the Mental Health Act that forced most of our mental institutions to put all the patients out onto the street that soon became the 600,000 homeless population of today. He reduced the tax rate on the wealthy from 72 percent to 50 percent in 1981 which was a good thing; the wealthy folks had saved our bacon through the previous 35 years by paying down the debt and it was time for them to get a break. But Reagan wasn't satisfied with a 22 percent cut and he turned around and reduced the rate on the wealthy another 12 percent to 38 percent two years later which caused him to have to borrow two and a half trillion dollars because of revenue shortfalls caused by the s tax cuts themselves. Reagan said on TV that having debt was a good thing for our nation! More poppycock!" The man with the dog said, "Yeah, it was just about that time when he deregulated the airlines and fired the12,000 PACO workers for going on strike, He hated unions!" … "Yes, he did, and he then got in over his head with the Iran-Contra Deal when he authorized U.S. agents to sell spare parts for surface to air Hawk missiles for $35 million. These were the missiles that the U.S. had sold to Iran in the 70's when the Shah was in power. It was evident during the congressional hearings that Ollie North really didn't know the money had made its way into a Swiss bank account for CIA Director Bill Casey. He broke down and admitted that he was told it was going for medical supplies for the Contras; oddly, CIA Director Bill Casey died several days later in Walter Reed Hospital. The investigation concluded that Bill Casey intended on using these funds for some of his Black Ops programs. Reagan should have been impeached! He was in bed with Casey!" … "Yeah, and he went along with those that managed the military industrial complex didn't he?" ... He sure did!

I continued, "The debt was just under a $1 trillion dollars when Reagan took office and it was almost $3 trillion when he left. There was only one billionaire when he took office; there were 51 when he left. The wages for the middleclass only rose 2.8 percent in eight years!" … "I remember that!" … "HW Bush and Clinton did okay in keeping the debt down and then along came GW who was a runaway spending disaster when it came to fiscal responsibility and he ran the debt up 300 percent to $11.8 trillion before he left office. Obama didn't add to the debt in spending, nevertheless, it costs over $400 billion a year to service the interest on the debt plus $2 trillion for the Financial

Meltdown Relief packages which grew the debt to $19 trillion eight years later when he left office." The man with the dog said, "What can we do about it now? They're not about to let go of their cash cow and stop supporting the wealthy and corporations and we're never going to be able to pay down this debt." … "Oh, I wouldn't bet on that for I believe the next generation of millennials could do it if they created a new party which would give us an active four party system that could enact laws to have a balanced budget, tax the wealthy 50 percent until the debt is back down to zero, and get our Military Industrial Complex right sized!" … "Wouldn't that be great!"

The dog had held its bladder long enough and was pulling hard on the leash, "Guess we better go. I really enjoyed talking to you. Off they went and I looked up into the Heavens, "How'd we do?"

I got to thinking after he left that some of the average middleclass workers who did vote for Reagan were unable to equate any of this with fairness for they too were hoodwinked and went eight years only getting a 2.8 percent increase in wages. During this same period Reaganonomics did in fact create 51 billionaires, 100,000 more millionaires and 10,000 deca millionaires.

Reagan deregulated the airlines with a stroke of the pen leaving the airlines scrambling for cash that was no longer coming from government subsidies. No longer were we able to buy an airline ticket that could be transferred between airlines because now the airlines had to use every trick in the bag to make money or go out of business. Reagan was a grandstander in Washington DC as he had been in Hollywood; quick with the comical quips and slow on common sense. Deregulating the airlines needed to take place, but not overnight. He could have spelled out a 10 year de-regulation program which would have allowed most of the airlines to stay in business and kept the public from getting scalped when traveling! That's what happens when we don't evaluate the persons and their policies before we elect them for presidents!

The first order of business for the Trump Administration was a tax cut for the nation which everyone knew was really for the wealthy folks that included a small tax reduction over ten years for the middleclass. How does Trump sleep at night after he spent a year campaigning to mid-stream America promising there'll be no tax cut for the wealthy only to turn around on his first week in office to announce a tax cut designed to enrich the wealthy? The GOP tax cuts are always added to the debt because the taxes from the rest of us cannot meet the budget; the debt at this writing is $27 trillion dollars with no discussions taking place whatsoever on how we intend to pay the debt down. The debt increased $7 trillion over 7 years under Obama and $8 trillion in four years under Trump. We don't have to be very smart to figure out that we are being played. Since 1981, the interest on the debt has grown 1670% to where we have paid $7.6 trillion dollars just for interest, and that in and of itself would be enough to pay the entire annual budget for two years or the Defense budget for ten years. It would also pay all our medical bills for 15 years or pay the college tuition for every student in the U.S. for 20 years. Voters that do not understand this should not be allowed to vote!

When Christine LaGarde, Head of the World Bank was asked in 2013 what she thought was the world's number one financial problem in the world she answered without a pause, "The U.S. debt!" which was half of what it is now!

We the People were acting fiscally responsibly under the Democrats and Republicans from 1945 to 1980 paying down the national debt until Reagan took power and declared having debt was good for the country. Those of you that don't believe any of this have only to get online and read the history of the National Debt and the Congressional budget!

Some of you will ask what's this got to do with what's been going on for the last four years? For starters, if your local or state government operated like this, they would have had to declare bankruptcy and maybe even have had to surrender or sell off parts of their state to bordering states at a land auction. Most world powers tax their citizens at a fair ascending rate in order to collect the necessary revenues to stay within their annual budget; it's that simple. Folks making over a million dollars a year should pay 50% income tax; the wealthy in Europe are taxed 65%. It's not thataway in the U.S. and it's not fair by any stretch. We are paying $500 billion dollars to borrow money to cover the revenue shortfall in the budget because the tax rate for the wealthy is too low. The debt clock is going to keep on ticking until one day the holders of our T-bills will want their money and the banks will no longer lend us more money to pay them. We will lose our AAA rating and if you think times are bad now, then you really have been living in a dream bubble. We must get fiscally responsible; remember, this is not a game of Monopoly and this is not the politician's money; it's ours!

Chapter 9

European countries have always been at odds with each other from the beginning of time whereas we've tried to have a live and let live policy with everyone not wanting to get caught up in any of their wars that never seemed to settle any of their long lasting resentments anyhow. Our American attitude of laissez-faire in this shrinking world didn't fare well with us or our neighbors because we never had an inkling as to who was telling us the truth and by the time we did get involved and took sides, the truth no longer mattered.

America was fast becoming a kaleidoscope of immigrants from all over the globe, but mostly from Europe. Whenever there was any kind of conflict or turmoil back in their homeland, they expected America to step in and do something about the injustices, but wisely enough, we almost always passed for we knew we'd always be at war.

Immigrants weren't welcomed in the communities until they spoke our language and their first generation of children were born here.

Latinos that came here in droves during the 1990's were not pressured into speaking English or learning our ways like previous immigrants. The U.S. Govt. made a disastrous error when they enacted legislature that pressured the states and the federal government to print documents and signs in Spanish hoping this would help the immigrants. This was a grave mistake for it caused most Americans to put the Latino immigrants into a negative light from the git-go that has lasted to this very day!

We as a nation knew that all immigrants were brave souls and had little wealth when they arrived. They were though bringing hundreds and hundreds of years of experience in carpentry, stone masonry, metal works, construction, languages, wisdom, and the arts.

If immigrants were as unlucky as the Irish were to arrive here around 1861, they were conscripted into the Union Army to fight in the Civil War. Some of the Italians arrived from the heavily controlled Costra Nostra crime areas in Sicily and Italy. It didn't take long for them to set up shop in the metropolitan areas and begin enforcing protection schemes on their own countrymen who had opened their own businesses. It took a hundred years for them all to get settled in, but not without a great deal of pain and hardship. Of course, while all of this was going on in the East, thousands of brave souls headed west to settle in areas that were unknown to anyone.

Word traveled fast around the globe about this new land with opportunities for everyone and people from everywhere around the globe were welcomed. Our cities turned into homogenous communities that were fast becoming an international fabric and not remotely similar to the Puritan or so called waspy fabric we once were when all this began in the 17th century.

The South never did get to begin its reconstruction after the Civil War, mostly because they were still smarting at having lost the war, were blaming all of their troubles on the Yankee carpetbaggers, and of course the negroes, some of who had now become tenant farmers were eking out a better existence than some of the poor whites. Some southern whites developed a Jim Crow attitude over the blacks which exacerbated an already explosive situation. Many white folks in the South never had to do any of the work that black folks did for 150 years and now they had no choice if they wanted to survive! What went around had come around!

John Garfield, our 20th president planned on developing a Reconstruction Plan for the South after he was elected president. He was gravely wounded during an assassination attempt four months after taking office and died eleven weeks later at age 49 leaving the South to remain in ruins and behind the times for another 40 years; it was almost a curse!

President Wilson saw fit for the U. S. to enter WW I in 1917 causing many southerners and northerners to be drafted into the Army. It may have been just what we needed for the North and South might have otherwise been two separate countries; one still living in the past and the other 50 years into the industrial age. The Treaty of Versailles which the U.S. did not sign, ended World War I and forbid Germany from having a large standing army or arsenals.

FDR was president when Adolph Hitler was coming into power. The world was still trying to dig itself out of the Depression of 1929 and times were lean. Twenty five percent of Americans were still unemployed as was the case in most of Europe. Hitler used these times and propaganda to get his fellow Germans riled up to where he became 'Their Fuhrer'. He went ahead and conscripted tens of thousands of men into the service for six months terms. After training they returned back to civilian life with their weapons and uniforms and remained fit and until they were recalled. It was obvious that he was preparing for war.

The USA was none the wiser until General Billy Mitchell returned from a visit to Europe and released the news that it was only a matter of time until Hitler released the dogs of war onto Europe; he was court martialed and held in disgrace! The Japanese joined Hitler and Mussolini and the three were now known as the Axis Powers. Japan had become the greatest naval power in the Pacific and the GOP continued to hold tight on the isolationist reins preventing FDR from strengthening our military which was politics at its worse.

The GOP continued their support of the isolationist movement that prevented FDR from getting congress or the senate to approve funds to update our naval fleets, Army, and Army Air Force; it was a dangerous and political game of wait and see. Political because the GOP used every tactic or trick in the book to take the opposing tack to whatever FDR proposed which caused America to lose eight precious years that we could have at least been using to upgrade our defenses knowing the world was heading into another war that surely would involve the USA. This is that part of the GOP that continues to be so terribly small minded and self-serving right up to today only they call this conservativism!

It's in these darkest of times that the actions of the American leaders were suspect, although who could blame the population for not wanting to have anything to do with what was going on in Europe and the Pacific. Nevertheless, FDR pushed on until one day an admiral of the Navy introduced FDR to Lt. Commander Arthur McCollum who was raised by his missionary parents in Japan right after the turn of the 20th century. On October 7, 1940 , he showed FDR an eight point strategy that would force the Japanese to attack the U.S. Fleet in the Pacific.

FDR implemented this strategy and on December 7th , 1941, the Japanese fleet did in fact attack Pearl Harbor sinking several battle ships and killing over 3000 men. We were finally in the war and this unsavory deed may have saved the world from tyranny; it was craftiness at its best, although if the GOP could have proved it, they surely would have impeached, imprisoned and maybe even had FDR and his entire administration shot! The world owes McCollum a debt of gratitude the likes beyond anything we can imagine!

The isolationist movement was nothing more than political grandstanding by the GOP to prevent FDR from gaining any more popularity after the Great Depression which was attributed to poor fiscal and investment oversight by the previous GOP administrations which was also the cause of the Great Recession in 2008. I sincerely doubt America would have stood the task of saving the world if it been up to the GOP, for they were totally myopic when it came to thinking of others and did not have the mindset let alone the strategic know how of FDR to gather the resources and prepare for the military complications that were about to come front and center for the U.S.; just look at how they managed the Covid-19 virus.

The ward bosses of St. Louis took control of the Democratic Convention in 1944 and informed FDR who was running for the 4th time, that the Democratic Party was not going to nominate him if he kept Henry Wallace as his VP. FDR conceded knowing this was a dastardly political act and one that still stands out as one of the worst blunders by the Democratic Party for there was no way HST would be welcomed into FDR's inner circle let alone be an asset to FDR. FDR died in April 1945 leaving Harry Truman, the haberdasher from Missouri the next president of the U.S.

The world was asleep at the wheel when North Korea, a pawn of the Russian and Chinese communists, invaded South Korea in June of 1950. Russia, China, and N. Korea gambled that the United States and the UN might not have the stomach for another war and they were close to being right. It was clear to Gen. Macarthur who had not set foot on the U.S. mainland since 1935, that the N. Korean army was going to drive the UN forces into the sea in Pusan when he asked for and received a reluctant nod from Truman and the Joint Chiefs to proceed with his recovery plan. In September 1950, the U.S. landed five divisions of troops, mechanized artillery, and tanks at Inchon which was just above Seoul and cut the N. Korean peninsula in half, relieved the siege on our troops in Pusan, captured 135,000 N. Korean troops, and pushed the remaining North Korean forces north across the Yalu River into China.; it ranks as one of the most brilliant tactical maneuvers in history and one that also should have ended the war had anyone except HST been president!.

I would suspect Gen. Macarthur felt it was a dark day in history when FDR met with Stalin at Yalta in 1945 just before he died in April 1945, and gave Stalin the keys to retain control of all the European countries that his Russian armies had recaptured from Hitler's armies. Churchill was aghast as well and could not believe what FDR had done. I'm of a mind that Gen. Macarthur was still upset about all of this and knew this moment in time after the Inchon Landing was going to be the only chance for the U.S. to reset what FDR did at Yalta. Macarthur may also have hoped that the U.S. upper command saw this as our only chance to put the USSR which was only months away from testing their first atomic bomb, back in the box , free all of Europe, and curtail China's plans to take over Asia at the same time. The U.S. had hundreds of B-36's loaded with nuclear bombs with which to deliver a nuclear knockout blow to Russia if they were to refuse pulling all their armies back into Russia.

Well, this is not what happened and I'm not about to play the devil's advocate with regard to HST who was always saying, "The buck stops here". It's always easy to make a judgement call the day after a game. HST was not a military tactician and he damn sure was not going to go to war on his watch and that in of itself probably saved us from killing millions of Russians and Chinese with our weapons of mass destruction. It might also been a sign that we were not acting for the higher good. The USSR and the U.S. did however enter into a Cold War that put the world into a state of the jitters for 30 years, cost us over 12 trillion dollars of our national wealth, and who knows, some may say we're all the better for it. It's what can happen when some political ward bosses in St. Louis used their self-serving politics to promote a haberdasher into a high stakes tactical arena with players who had the military intelligence and balls to finish off Germany , Italy, and Japan in WW II. Douglas MacArthur would have at least won the Korean War if HST could have suffered his impertinence.

HST fired Gen. Macarthur for voicing disparaging remarks to the press about HST not letting him continue to bomb the Chinese staging areas across the Yalu who were only waiting for the U.S. to blink, and we did. HST stopped the bombing, the Chinese troops crossed the Yalu River in November

1951 and drove our troops back to the 38th Parallel killing over 30,000 of our troops on the way; another dark day for America.

After this setback, Eisenhower had no trouble defeating Truman in the 1952 election and was president when the U.S. signed the Truce with N. Korea that put the Korean War on hold until this very day. We had just fought and won a war that should've ended all wars and HST and his politicians did not have the political mettle, will, know how, or courage to inform the people of what was at stake ergo we the people did not have the impetus to win the war! HST agreed to support the UN Police Action in Korea in June 1950, but lacked the grit to stay the course and let our generals win which cost 54,000 American soldiers their lives.

And yet, we were hoodwinked by these same actors into keeping 40,000 U.S. combat troops and equipment in South Korea that cost us over $2B a year or $135B for the next 66 years to show the world how we had the backs of the South Korean people, but not our own! What good does it do us to have a military industrial complex if our leaders don't have the mettle or intelligence on how to use it or does it even matter to the corporations running the military complex?

Chapter 10

Eisenhower won the election in 1952 and he along with Richard Nixon his Vice President gave the nod to the CIA to proceed with clandestine measures to overthrow Prime Minister Mossadegh of Iran in 1953 while we were still at war in Korea! Remember, the CIA, U.S. military, and three million workers in the military complex were mostly aligned and under the watchful eye of the GOP. I can tell you from firsthand knowledge that the Iranian citizens were not about to forgive America for this coup when I was working there ten years later; and why should they? How would we feel if someone came here from another country and covertly set into motion a plan that removed our president from office?

And let us not forget the beginnings of the unforgettable Vietnam War that were ongoing when Eisenhower took office in January 1953, and by 1954, the United States was providing almost 80 percent of the costs in weapons to keep the French in power in Vietnam. The Chinese communists were no longer bogged down in Korea and were able to supply the Vietnam communists with huge amounts of military weapons at the battle of Dienbienphu in 1954. Many UN nations viewed France as wanting to maintain their colonial hold on Vietnam. Gen. Ridgeway was against us getting involved for he knew the U.S. would need to send a half million troops there just to stop the siege at Dienbienphu. Eisenhower decided not to get involved and stopped further assistance to the French, but that didn't stop John Dulles, his Secretary of State from pushing his radical Domino Theory which predicted the fall of all the Southeast Asia nations one by one to the communists if we didn't stop them.

President Dwight D. Eisenhower gave his farewell speech to the nation on January 17, 1961, wherein he spoke the followings words about the military industrial complex:

"Until the latest of our world conflicts, the United States had no armaments industry. American makers of plowshares could, with time and as required, make swords as well. But we can no longer risk emergency improvisation of national defense. We have been compelled to create a permanent armaments industry of vast proportions. Added to this, three and a half million men and women are directly engaged in the defense establishment. We annually spend on military security alone more than the net income of all United States corporations.

Now this conjunction of an immense military establishment and a large arms industry is new in the American experience. The total influence; economic, political, even spiritual is felt in every city, every Statehouse, every office of the Federal government. We recognize the imperative need for this development. Yet, we must not fail to comprehend its grave implications. Our toil, resources, and livelihood are all involved. So is the very structure of our society.

In the councils of government, <u>we must guard</u> against the acquisition of unwarranted influence, whether sought or unsought, by the military-industrial complex. The potential for the disastrous rise of misplaced power exists and will persist. We must never let the weight of this combination endanger our liberties or democratic processes. We should take nothing for granted. Only an alert and knowledgeable citizenry can compel the proper meshing of the huge industrial and military machinery of defense with our peaceful methods and goals, so that security and liberty may prosper together."

He didn't mince his words when he said, "unwarranted influence … only an alert and knowledgeable citizenry can compel the proper meshing of the huge industrial and military machinery of defense with our peaceful methods and goals, but most importantly, don't forget his words, "We annually spent more for our defense than the net income of all United States corporations and now we spend more than all the other nations of the world combined spend for their defense"

When he said, "Only an alert and knowledgeable citizenry (that would be us), I will bet a year's salary that 99 percent of Americans know nothing about the GOP connection and involvement with the U.S. Military Industrial Complex! Yet, we are the ones that have to use due diligence to ensure we separate the truth from fiction which we all missed when we were bamboozled into the Vietnam War in 1964. We need to be aware of the goings on in and around the military industrial complex, for the military type industrial corporations will use their money, guile, and outright lies to control the political forces in our system of government in order to achieve that which may be good for them, but not necessarily good for us which is why this has been a political cash cow for the GOP Party for the last 60 years.

President Isenhower was Commanding General of all allied military forces in the Europe during WW II. He knew and appreciated the advantage of having an overwhelming arsenal, ships, aircraft, artillery, and weapons in the field.

....

Fidel Castro defeated Fulgencio Batista who had been dictator of Cuba from 1952 to 1959.

Fidel was invited to come to New York for a ticker tape parade in his honor, but before he came he secretly met with a delegation from Russia to discuss creating ties with Russia that would protect Cuba from a U.S. invasion that was sure to come; he was right. The CIA and Joint Chiefs were looking at all their options including making a preemptive strike against Cuba using the excuse that they wanted to recover corporate losses and damages after Castro nationalized all the American companies in Cuba. More importantly, the GOP had no doubts that VP Richard Nixon would beat JFK in the 1960 election and follow through with this invasion. JFK was the winner of the 1960 election and he was of no mind to conduct an invasion into Cuba. He was however blindsided from the underhanded behavior of the previous administration that had not advised him of their poorly planned Bay of Pigs invasion that ended up being a huge embarrassment for JFK right after he took office. He later replaced the CIA Director, Allen Dulles and froze any and all discussions with the CIA and Joint Chiefs on anything related to Cuba until a U-2 flight over Cuba took photographs of several ICBM missile batteries being constructed in October of 1962 that changed everything.

JFK announced to the world what was in play and began having conversations with Premier Khruschev who was a wily negotiator. JFK initiated a naval blockade on Cuba to prevent more Russian ships from bringing shipments to

Cuba. Every B-52 the U.S. had was in the air 24/7 being refueled and ready to carry out attacks against Russian targets.

The U.S. Joint Chiefs pleaded with JFK around the clock to let them bombard the missile site and invade the island; JFK wouldn't budge.

When the Russian ships approached the embargo, a U.S. destroyer fired several shots across the bow of the first ship and the Russian ships turned about. The world let out a gasp of relief and the United States and Russia began standing down.

After the USSR imploded in 1990, we learned from several retired high level Russian military staff officers that there were four Russian nuclear subs in the area that day and one of them tried to launch nuclear tipped torpedoes against the U.S. fleet but couldn't because one Russian naval officer, Vasili Arkhipov would not put in his code. Unknown to the U.S., they also informed us that they had set up four tactical nuclear missile batteries on the coast and would have launched these missiles had the U.S. attacked the Russian missile site or invaded Cuba; we would have plunged into a nuclear holocaust were it not for JFK's bullheaded steadfastness not to strike Cuba … talk about the blindsightedness of the U.S. Military vs the Grace of God!

JFK created what became known as the Green Berets and sent 6,000 of them to South Vietnam to train the South Vietnam troops. In December 1962, JFK sent Senator Majority Leader Mike Mansfield to Viet Nam on a two week fact finding mission and he advised JFK when he returned not to get further involved and to find an exit strategy out of

South Vietnam asap. At this stage, the U.S. troops were still only acting in an advisory or training capacity.

So, we have the Korean case where HST was not willing to seize the moment and another where the entire Joint Chiefs of Staff were prevented from having their way by the steadfastness of President Kennedy who ended up saving the world. Colin Powell said, **"Leadership is the art that accomplishes more than scientific management says is possible."**

On November 22, 1963, JFK was brutally assassinated in Dallas, Texas. The following day his wife Jackie hugged Robert Kennedy in Washington DC and said to him, "<u>They</u> murdered my husband!" Jackie wasn't as naive as we were!

There were many top level people in Washington in 1963 that knew JFK was secretly creating an exit strategy knowing there were high level military and CIA officials that did want to go to war. Lyndon B. Johnson his VP became the 36th president of the United States. Many in the JFK family blamed him for pressuring JFK into going to Dallas knowing Texas was a hot bed of anti JFK Republicans. LBJ lacked the quality of being his own man and it wasn't long before those same powers in Washington began pulling on his sleeve to get involved with Vietnam until it became a reality after several staged incidents that got the public aroused and lined up behind them.

A Russian official said Nikita Khrushchev became very emotional when he received word that JFK had been assassinated; they truly did respect each other.

Why is this story so important today? It's important because we have yet to come to terms with who the 'they' were that Jackie was referring to in order for us to see how a handful of hateful Americans, rogue CIA operatives, military interlopers, and God only knows how many licentious and self-serving officials took it upon themselves to join together and carry out a coup against a sitting president of their country. They were the lowest of the low for setting aside their sacred oaths; duty, honor, country and carrying out an ambush of a duly elected president because he interfered with their personal, political, irresponsible, and self-serving far right ill-advised military complex agendas. JFK found them objectionable, and knew they undermined the very fabric of what we as a nation stood for in what can only be described as the darkest of our times that finally led all of them to murder him in the streets of Dallas.

....

In 1964, President Johnson announced on TV that an incident had just taken place in the Gulf of Tonkin wherein the USS Maddox destroyer was attacked by three North Vietnam Navy torpedo boats and the Maddox expended almost 300 3" and 5" shells.

In 2005, an internal National Security Agency historical study was declassified. It concluded that the *Maddox* had engaged the North Vietnamese Navy on August 2, but that there were no other North Vietnamese naval vessels present during the incident of August 4. The report concluded there were no incidents on either August 2 or August 4; they had both been staged to get national attention and were to be used to get us involved in the Vietnam War. A total disgrace to the CIA, the US Navy, the U.S. Pentagon, and LBJ, the president of the U.S. that led to 51,000 U.S. servicemen dying in an unnecessary war; JFK was right and he was murdered because he wanted no part of what the GOP and military industrial complex were up to. This is what happens when we the people don't do our homework to ensure we are sending the very best to Washington DC.

The lesson for us is that there are still many so called patriots in our nation today with like-minded dark ideas on how they should be running our country that need to be tethered on a short leash and let us not forget the advice of President Eisenhower that demands we compel the proper meshing of the huge industrial and military machinery of defense with our peaceful methods and goals, in other words, we must never take our eyes off them, the self-proclaimed patriots, and we should never, ever let down our guard down .

Chapter 11

You might be asking what Israel, Cuba, Iran, and Iraq might have to do with what's been going on for the last four years. Plenty, if you consider many of todays issues stem from some of our past leaders not acting with honor or not making formal apologies or not putting appropriate closure on issues that continue to linger on to today; and we all know what happens when we don't put closure on something.

The first of these apologies would be to the Palestinian people. In 1939, the German liner St. Louis anchored off of Miami waiting for the U.S. Immigration Department or President Roosevelt to allow the 1200 or so Jews on the ship to enter into the U.S. who otherwise would end up in German death camps when the ship returned to Germany. Hitler wanted to prove to the world that no country wanted Jews to immigrate into their country. He was right; the ship ultimately did return to Germany and the Jews were transported to the death camps. This weighed heavy on some American consciences after the war to where our leaders supported Jewish immigrants from everywhere in Europe making their way to Palestine after having survived the holocaust which was more about guilt and sympathy than it was compassion, and for sure they still didn't want them coming here. But did anyone ask what right did we or any other nation have to make such a proposition? Palestine was a sovereign nation and they had no say in the matter.

The Balfour Conference was held in 1917 followed by the Cairo Conference in 1921. Both conferences were held by the British who were the custodians overseeing the breakup of the Ottoman Empire, namely to determine the future of

Palestine since it was no longer a part of the Ottoman Empire because the Ottoman Empire no longer existed. The terms from both of these conferences were explicit in that the Palestinians would have self-rule in Palestine and Palestine would be a free state. It just so happens there were 10,000 Jews living peacefully with the 700,000 Palestinians at the time.

The disbelief that the Palestinians experienced when the British evoked the Edict of Partition in 1947 that split Palestine into two states had to have numbed their psyche. They knew they were not going to be able to win a war against the Jews who were receiving astronomical financial aid from every Jewish community throughout the world; especially from America. The Jewish lobby put pressure to bear on U.S. leaders until they adopted UN Rule 181 in 1948 that allowed partition of Palestine and the rest is history. The Palestinians fought to retain their country but they were out gunned and outmatched due to overwhelming financial support from the Jews and sympathizers in America. Palestine went from being a sovereign nation, to one being split in two and then into one country called Israel that had power over everyone. This was a world tragedy that should never have ended like this. The British were in charge of the breakup of the Ottoman Empire and they could have just as easily created a Jewish state on the Sinai Peninsula; shame on them. This was beyond not being a fair shake for the Palestinians by any sense of the word. That was seventy two years ago and a great deal of blood has flowed since then. It was the UN's, Britain's, and America's darkest moment in the Middle East, the world did not hold Jews in a good light, and after this debacle they were held in contempt!

A nuclear materials processing factory in Apollo, Pennsylvania managed by Israeli scientists that made weapon grade materials for the U.S. Navy was suspected of stealing and shipping some of these weapon grade materials to Israel during the late 1950's and early 1960's. Admiral Rickover met with JFK and informed him of what he suspected was going on, however, JFK was assassinated before he could determine if this was in fact the truth, and there are those to this day that say this may have led to his assassination.

Arab countries throughout the Middle East didn't agree with how Israel ended up erasing Palestine from the world map and used every opportunity to undermine Israel to where the Six Day War broke out in 1967. The U.S. had an Intel ship called the USS Liberty on station fifteen miles off of the Egyptian coast listening to Israeli and Egyptian battlefield communications. They heard and recorded Israel generals giving orders to their commanders on the Sinai Peninsula not to take any prisoners. For two days Israeli Mirage fighters attacked and tried to sink the USS Liberty with 172 sailors that resulted in the killing of 34 American sailors and wounding 100 others.

U.S. destroyers rescued and towed the ship from harm's way to safety. Israel vehemently denied the accusations until recorded communications of the fighter pilots did reveal that they were in fact trying to sink this unarmed ship of their ally, the United States. Israel offered a payment of $20,000 to each of the dead sailors' families which most families considered an insult.

Israel secretly detonated a below ground nuclear device in South Africa in 1972, and we, meaning the United States of

America whose leaders had hoped this incident would never see the light of day, never said another word for they knew where they got the fissionable material. Most Americans I've talked to personally do not see Israel as our friend or ally; Israel only looks out for Israel. Worse and foremost, so much for the U.S. military complex making sure our nuclear weapons did not fall into another country's hands.

On November 27, 2020, 24 days after the election, Iran announced that their chief nuclear scientist was killed by an Israeli hit team in Iran yesterday. I for one do not believe Israel would ever want to jeopardize the $3 billion stipend they receive from the U.S. every year by not getting the nod from President Trump on this caper. I also don't know why we Americans think Israel has been our friend over the last 75 years since we've caught 75 Israeli secret agents spying and stealing our secrets, and yet, we continue to send Israel $3 billion a year, why? We all know why; some of our insecure leaders are still afraid of the powerful Jewish lobby! Deplorable! Palestine receives the paltry sum of $500 million a year in financial assistance from the U.S.

There is no way an Israeli agent would have dared to take out this famous Iranian scientist without a nod from the U.S. although strange things can happen when we have a lame duck president and his Jewish son in-law who may have wanted to let Israel have its way.

The Palestinian and Israel conflict will continue until Israel at a minimum agrees to restore all the land boundaries established in the UN Resolution 181 of 1948 to their original locations and vacates all their expansion settlements in the West Bank. The only way for this to happen is for countries throughout the world to start closing their borders to Israeli commerce, tourists, and visitors; there's power in numbers! This travesty has gone on long enough and Israel will not stop expanding their settlements into the West Bank until their way of life becomes threatened. The UN hasn't had the integrity or the courage to repair what should never have happened in the first place.

. . . .

The case with Iran is so similar to what happened when the GOP in 2001 turned a blind eye to GW Bush's administration wanting to launch an invasion into Iraq. When Paul O'Neill, GW Bush's first Secretary of the Treasury took notes during GW Bush's first cabinet meeting on January 21, 2001, he captured what was foremost on GW Bush's agenda. After everyone had been introduced to each other GW said something to the affect, "What are we going to do about Iraq?" Paul remembered each of the cabinet members looking bewilderedly at one another. GW's father, HW Bush had put Saddam Hussein back into the box when he unleashed 450,000 U.S. troops into Iraq during the Desert Storm War in 1991 after Iraq invaded Kuwait and there was no way Saddam wanted any more trouble with the U.S. military. So, why would GW want to mention this on his first day in office ... the only thing I can come up with is that he either wanted to do a one up on his father, or he and Cheney were going after the oil in Iraq.

GW as he was known amongst his family and friends had always seen himself as being a few steps ahead of everyone and soaring above the fray. He was able to avoid the draft and join the Air National Guard in 1968 when everyone knew there were 300 people ahead of him for the same posting. He became a F102 fighter pilot until he up and left his duty post in Montgomery, Alabama in May of 1972 and returned to Texas. He certainly had family connections to government and well-heeled petrochemical power that were going to be the guiding factors for him when he decided to make his move and run for the office of the president.

April 22, 2000, seven months before the presidential election in 2000, Janet Reno, U.S. AG at the time, sent Federal Marshals to the home where the young Cuban boy Elian Gonzales was staying with his relatives in Miami. The marshals took Elian into custody in order to return him to his father, who was his legal guardian and lived in Cuba. The Miami Cuban population demonstrated their anger by taking to the streets right through to election night. Most Cubans favored the Republicans because JFK would not satisfy their revenge for Castro and invade Cuba, but after this event, any Democrats that hadn't made up their minds surely switched their vote for GW Bush.

There were problems with the Palm Beach County ballots having chads and the Florida Supreme Court voted to allow a recount. Jim West, former Secretary of the Treasury for HW Bush got involved and ended up getting the U.S. Supreme Court to invalidate the Florida Supreme Court decision for a recount which then opened the way for West to get the Supreme Court to take a vote and they declared GW Bush a winner. Ruth Bader Ginsburg said that this was the lowest point in the history of the Supreme Court as they had no right or historical precedent to overrule a sovereign state. The U.S. Supreme Court denied the State of Florida's right to have a recount and went on to proclaim GW Bush the 43rd president of the United States. Without the recount,

GW won Florida by 459 votes but until there was a recount, who is to say. There is no doubt that when Janet Reno sent marshals to Miami she also caused what may have been thousands of Democratic voters who hadn't yet made up their minds to switch to the GOP candidate. No one on this earth would have ever connected the dots of those two events in a million years, however, when Elian Gonzales' mother got the thought to escape to the U.S. from Cuba in a raft with her son Elian, that's exactly what happened? This otherwise obscure event set into motion who would became the next president of the U.S. and the idea that GW would subsequently order a military invasion into Iraq was beyond being incomprehensible. Are we to believe that there are times when some benevolent or malevolent force can split the veil and alter events that otherwise were not going to occur; is this what is meant by happenstance? If it is, this would suggest that when Elian's mother got the idea to escape from Cuba in a raft with her son to the United States, the Universe was setting into motion events that would have repercussions of monumental magnitude; hard to believe but not impossible.

I for one doubt GW Bush would have won the presidency had Janet Reno waited until the election was over to take Elian Gonzales into custody and because she didn't, it led to 500,000 Iraqis and 4000 Americans losing their lives along with the wasting of two trillion dollars of our national wealth. Goes to show you what can happen when someone among us has what would seem to be a most benign thought, the results of which could create a tiny obscure event that could change the entire course of history, and yet, not change most of us at all!

9/11 happened and it took three months for the Bush administration to put together a force of 38,000 soldiers to go into Afghanistan and comb the Boro-Boro mountains looking for Osama bin Ladin for almost two years with no significant additional forces added forthwith. The Bush administration made a decision not to invade Afghanistan and capture Osama bin Ladin who had planned and carried out the attack on the United States because this would have interfered with his plans to invade Iraq. Osama bin Ladin himself was an offspring of the Royal Saudi family who I might add were somewhat close friends with the Bush family. How this played out we may never know because oil sometimes is much thicker than blood. Still, Osama bin Ladin was responsible for carrying out the attack that killed 3000 civilians in the World Trade Center on September 11, 2001 and this event got in the way of GW and his band of irresponsible marauders; Cheney, Rumsfeld, Wolfowitz, and Feith, to invade Iraq. GW's mission was to convince the world that there were WMD (weapons of mass destruction) in Iraq so he could have his way in Iraq.

We all know what happened when Secretary of State Colin Powell realized he'd been played by the Bush cabinet and was smugly dubbed the 'Reluctant Warrior" when he no longer supported GW's premise that there were WMD's in Iraq. Of course, once GW had the support from Congress it didn't matter who was on board. GW had permission to unleash a preemptive attack on a country that had not provoked us or done anything to deserve it, and for the first time in our history we made a preemptive invasion of another country; Iraq! We all sat in our living rooms wondering how could this be happening, and yet, there had been no effort to launch an attack similar to that of Desert

Storm against Afghanistan where the attack on the World Trade Center had been conceived and carried out from. Are you all still with me?

The irresponsible marauders decided on a military operation that was going to be on the cheap thinking Saddam Hussein was in no shape to withstand another military invasion. That may have been true, but this was not where they made their big mistake. They failed to take into account as did HW Bush did in 1991 during Desert Storm of who was really in charge in Iraq and they didn't have a clue how the multiple Islamic factions and tribal ethnicities when ruptured would be the dominant factor on who was going to win or lose. They didn't do their homework to see who the principal players were going to be when this was over and how all of these things would lead to their demise. There was no way the Sunnis who had been in power for 75 years were going to roll over and fade away knowing that they had enough weapons and munitions buried all over Iraq to rearm ten armies.

In an effort to pacify Sunni resistance, GW authorized five (5) C5A cargo plane shipments of U.S. currency totaling 12 billion dollars sent to Baghdad for Bremer to use as counter weights for all the different players in the Iraqi establishment and we Americans did not let out a peep. To this day there has been no financial accounting as to who got <u>our</u> money which in and of itself was a criminal act.

The invasion also set off a series of tribal shifts throughout the entire Middle East out of which gave birth to Isis, the Syrian revolution, the Brotherhood takeover in Egypt, the collapse and failure of Libya, and the subsequent instability of the entire Middle East to this very day. The U.S. found itself in quicksand with upwards of 100,000 troops in Iraq without a goal or knowing what an exit strategy would even look like if it was handed to them. The timid GOP leaders on the hill conducted less than 20 Congressional oversight hearings a year on the Bush administration over eight years; the normal number would have been closer to four hundred; ring any bells!

Six hundred Iraqi civilians died and millions have been dislocated form their homes and their country since the U.S. invaded Iraq.

Can we still ask what has this to do with voting? Voters turned around in 2004 and gave GW Bush a 2nd term for which I have given the American voters an F- on that report card.

....

Like the Iraq catastrophe, the GOP had an off the cuff assessment of Cuba after finding fault with Fidel Castro for entering into a pact with Russia who was our primary adversary in 1959 that subsequently led to Russia setting up ICBM's (Intercontinental Ballistic Missiles) in Cuba to create a buffer to ensure the U.S. wouldn't invade or attack Cuba. How's that for good thinking? Imagine the U.S. finding fault with any country, especially our closest neighbor, Cuba, for doing what they needed to do to keep their neighbor, the U.S. from invading their homeland!

The GOP was being arrogant when they viewed Castro's approach of using any means possible including Russia to safeguard his homeland and when it happened they took it personal vs GW Bush who was just misbehaving, cocky, and acting grandiose. The GOP thought there was no way JFK could win the 1960 election for president and Eisenhower gave the nod for the Bay of Pigs invasion to move forward anyway. JFK won the election and Eisenhower did not inform JFK of their detailed planning to invade Cuba making this an embarrassment for JFK. The GOP should have been ashamed, embarrassed, or at least apologizing for not putting country first, but they weren't because they're not good at carrying out stealthy international operations or apologizing. So, yes, if we continue to elect leaders that fail to amend or apologize for their shortcomings, then we are left to live with their dastardly shortcomings for generations, and since we all have such short memories, vote them into power again.

So, it's not surprising that the Cuba issue has remained a thorn in the flesh for the GOP causing them to want to continue the trade embargo against Cuba for another thousand years all because of their own arrogance! President Obama saw fit to re-open a U.S. Embassy in Cuba in 2014 and remove trade and travel restrictions. Trump won the 2016 election and he reimposed travel and trade restrictions on Cuba if for no reason other than this is how he handled all of Obama's changes making this one of his greatest failings as president proving that we elected a 6 year old boy for our 45th president! I am hoping most of you are still on the train.

....

President Trump promised when he was campaigning for the presidency that he would pull the U.S. out of the Iran Nuclear Treaty if for no other reason than Obama was central to the creation of the treaty and anything Obama developed he planned on undoing if he did win the presidency unaware that he was just adding more problems to the Middle East. Why, because there is a cause and effect for every single policy shift in the Middle East no matter how miniscule.

No matter what anyone thinks of Iran, they did step up and agree to curb their nuclear weapons development programs and sign a treaty with six other nations that included China and Russia that allowed the IAEA (International Atomic Energy Association) to have access to all their nuclear experimental works and cameras at all these locations to ensure they did in fact honor the treaty.

The last two GOP presidents were dreadful tacticians when it came to handling military operations and international affairs especially when it came to wanting to bomb Iran for being a rogue regime. Truth is, there are many rogue regimes in the world and we must learn to live and let live with all of them. This was really all about GOP payback for Iran's revolutionaries kidnapping and holding 51 U.S. Embassy workers in 1979 for 451 days. The GOP hopes the light of day will never reveal their clandestine part in the CIA plot that led to the overthrow of Iran's President Mossadegh in 1953 which ultimately led to the return of Shah Pahlavi who in fact was a pawn of the U.S. This then opened the door for U.S. oil and weapon companies to do business in Iran, which ultimately led the Iranian revolutionaries to overthrow the Shah and the kidnapping of the 51 American Embassy workers. This was exactly what President Eisenhower was warning us about! You might be asking at this point what has all this got to do with what's going on over the last four years here at home … it has everything to do with what's going on at home because we continue to elect arrogant leaders that do not have the wherewithal to stop creating all of the events I have mentioned, and what is worse, we have not put closure on any of these events to this very day. As for Trump, he was totally out of his league when it came to the Middle East. He was wrong to move our embassy in Tel Aviv to Jerusalem which was an outright slap in the face of the hagiocracy government of Jerusalem that is made up of Christian, Islamic, and Jewish representatives that manage the affairs of the city. Again, the U.S. has become the fly in the ointment and we wonder why there is no peace in the Middle East!

The GOP couldn't wait to meet with Chinese leader Mao Tse Tung for 7 days in 1972 so they could open up trade negotiations that would benefit the large U.S. corporations (not the U.S. workers) that wanted to make huge windfalls of profit from the low priced labor and manufacturing costs in China. The GOP followed by ensuring that China could become a UN member. Just how were they up to all of this knowing the Chinese killed 30,000 U.S. soldiers when China decided to enter the Korean War in 1952. You are probably saying, 'This is all water under the bridge' and I say, 'whose bridge'? Cubans never did anything like this to us and the GOP won't even talk to them!

A simple public apology to the Iranians would have sufficed for carrying out a coup on their leader! A simple apology to the Cubans for supporting the Cuban dictator Baptiste in the 1950's, for turning a blind eye to all the U.S. gangsters that were running gambling casinos and whore houses for wealthy businessman in Cuba, not to mention the U.S. companies taking advantage of cheap Cuban labor would have accomplished wonders; ergo the GOP was indirectly responsible for Russia being invited to Cuba to set up ICBM sites.

I was overseeing the construction of a power plant project in Bolivia in 1999 and I had lunch with all the Bolivian engineers and office management team every day. I wanted to improve my Spanish speaking skills and the Bolivians wanted to improve their English speaking skills. It was grand!

One day one of the engineers said, "I was wondering what you thought of your country bombing the power plants in Serbia that was on TV last night? I was really caught of guard for we never talked about world politics. The engineer then said, "You know, the United States really frightens us because whenever they feel a country has done something wrong against them, they can just shoot cruise missiles at them from a ship hidden at sea ... what gives your country the right to act with such impunity around the world? The United States is not the world's policeman." The silence was deafening. There was nothing I could say or wanted to say and I'll bet Isenhower would not have wanted to answer this question as well!

Chapter 12

This racism and white supremacy business has been going on long before Trump arrived on the scene, but it would seem four years ago that those infected with racist ideas may have awoken and found a leader who has the same views and opinions of people of color as they do and now there is no longer a need for them to keep their dark thoughts and opinions under wraps.

Remember, our first mission here is to find out what are the issues that keep us apart. Do we or do we not have the mental acuity and spiritual fortitude to determine if a candidate will protect and honor our Constitution and conduct himself or herself in an honorable and democratic fashion? To simply say everyone should have the right to vote may not be acceptable although there are some of us who would demand they have a right to vote, or say you can't stop me or you can't make me to do this, or worse, I have a right to do whatever I want to do ... I'm sure these attitudes of today would have given the founders a fit!

I believe after all was said and done, they came to a conclusion that they could only justify putting the future of this newly won democracy in the hands of the educated people and found that only most of the land owners had some degree of education. Did they make the right decision knowing there will always be educated voters with radical tendencies?

Every other Monday when I was doing a project in Canada I would catch a flight on a small plane in Ottawa going to New Brunswick with single seating on each side. I recognized the pilots and stewardess from previous flights and they would gave me a wave. A few minutes before the stewardess closed the door she approached a man sitting a few rows down on the other side of the plane and talked to him. When she finished and returned to the galley, the man got up, gathered his things, and left the plane. When the stewardess passed by I asked her if the man was on the wrong plane, She said, "Oh no, he smelled terrible!' She could see from my expression that I was taken aback, "Really!" She knew I was an American and said, "I'm sure airlines in the states would never ask a person to leave a plane if they smelled as terrible as him ... you Yanks are so free that you are going to end up trespassing and crisscrossing over each other's boundaries with impunity until someone gets hurt; that's not the case here in Canada." I had to agree with her for I was pretty sure no stewardess in the U.S. would've asked him to leave the plane. She was right; we yanks are so full of our freedoms to do this or do that or whatever we wanted to do.

We all know that civilians cannot be ordered around like soldiers, but in some ways, we civilians are not that different from the sailors on a battleship. Some of the sailors on a battleship have different political and religious beliefs, and some even have their own tactical opinions which is okay but not okay to employ without permission from the Captain. And yet, the most important task they are all obligated to do is to have each other's back with no strings attached. This is not something that just sounds good; it's the only way the battleship can function. There can be no half measures! If some of the sailors aboard the ship began handing out political flyers to persuade sailors with other political and tactical beliefs to join their affiliation what would happen to the mission and the morale?

We civilians on the other hand are free to express our views and we should because it's our differences with one another that make the difference! There are hundreds of thousands if not millions of Americans right now that refuse to wear their masks that has resulted in hundreds of thousands more Covid infections and tens of thousands of deaths a month. What's worse is many are saying, "It's my right ... you cannot make me wear it." The CDC authorities have pinpointed the people who refuse to wear the masks as the culprits and have branded them as being irresponsible for spreading the disease.

The Covid-19 virus started in China and yet they managed to get it under control in twelve weeks' time because 100 percent of their people voluntarily were wearing masks 24/7. It's what they've been doing for the last 1000 years; they do not wait for the leaders in Beijing to tell them.

Ever wonder why is it that some Americans don't make a big deal when they are refused entry into a bar or tavern that has a sign on the door that reads, 'No shoes, no shirt, no service'. People who do not have shoes or shirts on will not be served and that's the end of it. Not so with those that refuse to wear a mask and some of them can become down right confrontational even though it has been proven that not wearing masks has already killed 260,000 Americans. So, what's going on! Arrogance!

Has anyone noticed that for first time in decades we have not had the normal annual flu epidemic this past year? We haven't because almost everyone has been wearing a mask, washing their hands, maintaining 6 feet distances from one another, and avoiding crowds.

Could it be political? How could they have more of an investment in Trump's political persuasions than wearing a mask that would definitely prevent them from spreading a disease that they may not even know they have that could kill their fellow Americans? Is this not reckless endangerment?

For starters, this never would have happened aboard the battleship I mentioned because they would be thrown into the brig and court martialed if they refused to wear their masks. Our authorities don't waste anytime declaring Martial Law after a hurricane or earthquake to prevent looting, so why wouldn't the authorities declare Martial Law during this Covid virus and mandate everyone must wear a mask as soon as they leave their home, office, or automobile, and if they don't, they would be arrested and charged with second degree reckless endangerment. We all know the answer to this question; if the governors and mayors mandate the wearing of masks in a GOP controlled state they will be recalled or primaried in the next election, but what's worse is they would rather expose their citizens to the virus than stand up to Trump. Therein lies the problem which means the GOP owns these deaths!

Have any of his supporters wondered why Trump behaves in such a contrary manner in all areas of his leadership. It's one thing to be your own man and it's another thing to be reckless. I've only seen Trump bend to one person since he's been elected president of the United States and that is Putin. It was obvious to everyone when Trump had just returned to the podium from their two hour meeting that he had been given his marching orders; couldn't his base see this? Are they so enthralled that they cannot see how he backed down to this man. Where was all that bravado he spewed at his rallies and debates? He surely didn't have it when he was at that podium in Helsinki did he? Why didn't his base pick up on this? Are the people in his base not able to see what happens to Trump when he is running with the hounds and sleeping with the foxes? Could they not see that he was cowering in the presence of someone who knew he had the upper hand? Are his supporters concerned how others might perceive them if they find Trump's behavior unobjectionable because if that's the case, this is a spiritual disorder as well as a psychiatric one.

The first word in the Declaration of Independence is We because those brave individuals from many walks of life with many aspirations and beliefs decided they no longer wanted to live under the boot of a king who had no personal interest in their welfare. That was and should always be the reason why We must have each other's back no matter who most of us think would be a better leader for us all or who would treat us better, or who is the right color, or who is the wisest, or who agrees or disagrees with us … We will perish as a nation if we fail to respect or consider each other's common welfare!

So, we find ourselves in one disagreement after another that I believe is no coincidence for we have become so divisively politicized over the last sixty years that we have unknowingly been played to where we have become patsies. What's worse is we each had to play our part in all of this in order for us to become patsies! That's what makes patsies hate the way they feel and this will continue with Trump's supporters until they finally admit that they too have been played and have become patsies ... they are complicit!

Webster's dictionary defines the word patsy as a person who is easily victimized, duped , manipulated, a pushover, a chump, pigeon, soft touch, or sucker. Sit for a spell and let these words soak in.

Each of us at times has been had! We've all had the best intentions and lost! So, what is it that makes us think we'll be okay if we split off into radical groups that think the same dark thoughts? Remember, it's our differences with one another that are going to make the difference! If you seek solace in a group that thinks the same as you, you may be giving up more of yourself than you know.

Political parties were developed to promote policies to achieve security, wealth, treaties, laws, healthcare, education, and economical success for its citizens. Over time, some of the citizens prospered more than others and they began wanting more control over the political party that had their best interest in mind which for them would be to increase and safeguard their wealth which resulted in the rest of us not having much of a say in all of this. An active four party system would allow us to restructure our tax code to resolve some of these issues.

In the meantime, we don't have to be math majors to know the party of the prosperous folks does not have enough people to vote for their candidates. This forces them to adopt less honorable messaging and tactics to attract and increase the number of members of their party to ensure they will have the necessary votes to elect their leaders and enact legislation that will assist them in achieving their goals which primarily are intended to safeguard and increase their wealth.

Even though there are more folks in the party of the common folk, the party of the wealthy seems to be able to attract enough voters during mid-term and national elections to get their candidates elected to the Presidency, Congress and the Senate. If that fails, they return to gerrymandering the configuration of the districts in key states to ensure the GOP has a majority of voters which will result in them controlling the electoral vote during a national election. The goal for both parties is exactly the same; power and policies to hold onto power! Neither party can achieve their party goals without having enough voters to ensure they can take control of the government and therein lies the slippery slate.

There are many white folks in our country that are not comfortable with people of color having affluence or influence in the political or social arenas and I'm not going to spend time trying to put a spin on this because this has been an issue since the beginning of our Republic; white people in the U.S. seem to have more of an investment in their skin color than people of color. I on the other hand have lived and worked in countries where 98 percent of the natives were of one color and they seem to have a live and let live attitude regarding skin color. I'm going to take a great leap and suggest that white people in countries with large numbers of people of different color, have become somewhat concerned and upset about competition. They're also very nervous that their race is going to be coming up behind those that they have up to now kept down and not been able to achieve their American Dreams. The movie Hidden Numbers is an excellent example of what white people are afraid of when it comes to skin color. And some whites are also uneasy when they see people of color having more children, are genuinely content, and happy as they can be as they make their way through this world.

The white race has ruled the Western hemisphere for millenniums and some of the more insecure whites are fast becoming nervous that the future white generations are going to be left behind or eased out. Remember, spirituality is the dominant factor in us humans and you have only to watch a church full of blacks on a Sunday morning to appreciate that they know they are being taken care of by a loving God who is watching over them. Amen!

So, back to the GOP party that is okay with us having a national debt nearing $27 trillion that requires an annual interest payment of $600 billion to service the debt. This is a grave and unsettling situation in our nation for two reasons. First, it's unfair! Secondly, if U.S. Treasury bond holders around the world start to think their money is not safe because of the U.S. debt being too high, then there goes our AAA bond rating. The U.S. dollar has been solid around the world for over a hundred years and don't think China and Russia wouldn't like to put a stop to this. So, why is it okay for the GOP to put all of us in harm's way just to cater to the wealthy? Because it's the only policy that has increased the wealth for the wealthy folks in their party that's why! So, lets return to the 'Haves' and the 'Have Nots' to see who is snookering who.

Do you have any idea how many kids could be educated for the $600 billion a year that we are paying in interest on this debt? We are the only country of the top 20 GDP countries that doesn't have some kind of national health and educational safety net. We are the only country with many of its population armed to the teeth by some who do not have the mental capacity to own or operate a weapon.

Between 1970 and 2020, 1283 children have been shot in our schools by other children who had access to automatic hand guns or military type assault weapons. The GOP party was and continues to be connected at the hip to the NRA (National Rifle Association) that supports the 2nd Amendment that says we Americans have a right to bear arms. The NRA advocates and supports all citizens having a right to purchase or own any type of automatic hand gun or assault rifle weapon of their choosing without having to have a federal or state permit or any background check. The NRA is really a lobby for the GOP Party and the gun control legislation is just a lot of smoke and mirrors to keep 8 million more voters in the GOP circle! The Senate has been under GOP control for the last 18 years and they have steered clear of any legislation that controls the sale or use of fire arms. Bearing arms and making it possible for people that should never have a gun are two very separate issues.

But they surely weren't all that patriotic back in 1973 when Richard Nixon, the GOP president who was about to resign for his part in the Watergate affair, signed into law the creation of the All-Volunteer Army. It was the darkest of moments for now the job of taking the fight to the enemy would only be accomplished by the marginalized or those who joined the service because of personal or economical pressures. The GOP ensured that their children and the children of the wealthy or powerful would no longer be required to have any skin in the defense of their country. No longer would everyone be comingling with men and women from all over the country that they otherwise were never going to meet, and worse, no longer would we all have each other's back in war and peace. So much for the GOP version of patriotism.

This All Voluntary Army removed that precious bond we all received when we all were drafted and comingled with one another that we otherwise never would have met. The most important benefits young men and women received when they entered the service is learning how to work and interface with others not of their choosing and becoming adults which for me was one of the greatest adventures of my life. Thank you, Uncle Sam!

I hope you're still with me, but you're not going to like this either; patsies become patsies because they don't pay attention! The advent of the computer age in the 80's and the smart phones showing up after the turn of the century made matters worse and further complicated our social network by letting us think we had arrived! We've got this!

We're all tapping our fingers on the table waiting for all of this angst to go away; I believe it's going to get much worse before it gets better and the only way it's going to get better is if we each have everyone's back and <u>undivided</u> attention. We're going to have to make some hard choices for ourselves, our families, and our nation and we need adults to do this!

Patsies don't make very good adults or finding their way out of a maze, not to mention that they are also a gullible lot and like to wait until there is some kind of consensus. This won't work at all with what we're up against. We have to think out of the box, and thank God, we will have the information at our finger tips to do it (if they don't start erasing parts of history on the web) which is why it is so very important for each of us to become masters at finding out what's best for us and not waiting on the leader of the herd to start calling the shots. Moses meandered around the desert with his flock for forty years because they couldn't reach a consensus on where to go … sound familiar with where we've been for the last forty years?

This dedicated work that Lincoln talked about is our increased devotion to the hammering out this nation's shortcomings on the anvil of time. Only then do you truly have any skin in the game. It's the We doing that makes for the Us receiving!

We have to discern who are the best leaders to continue the great tasks that lie before us; not the charismatic or outlandish candidates that come and go that are nothing but a 'A Flash in the Pan'. The term flash in the pan is an expression from our colonial beginnings. It's what happens when the hammer on a rifle strikes the flint and ignites the powder in the pan, but doesn't ignite the powder in the chamber behind the bullet; all flash and no action! The only thing worse than having a leader who is a flash in the pan is their supporters who haven't figured any of this out.

There'll always be politicians that are blowing their own horns, puffed up by the office they hold that are quietly and steadfastly going about the business of making this into their business and we have to wise up and prevent this from happening lest we perish!

.

Chapter 13

When the Covid-19 virus first showed up in Wuhan, China, a city of 11 million people in November 2019, Chinese epidemiologists contacted the leaders in the Chinese government who immediately put the kybosh on any announcements to the public. However, U.S. Intelligence picked up on some of the behind the scene Chinese chatter and notified the National Security Council at the White House about the virus and it was placed in the PDB (Presidential Daily Brief), but because President Trump was known for not reading the briefs, we may have been put in harm's way.

President Trump did get on TV eventually and made some off the cuff comments in early February about the Chinese having some problems with a virus but that the people in the U.S. did not have to worry about it because it was just going to go away. A week later he stopped all air travel to and from China. It was two weeks later when the people of the U.S. knew they had been blindsided by their president, broadsided by the virus, left to think they did not have to maintain a safe distance from one another, chafed at having to wear a face mask because the president wasn't wearing one, did not have the necessary PPE (Personal Protective Equipment) for all the healthcare providers, and did not have the ventilators needed to care for the infected patients that were overwhelming the ER's and ICU's across the country. Our leadership was a disgrace!

The shelves that normally carried toilet paper, paper towels, and disinfectant sprays in the super markets and drug stores were bare. Some stores had limits of one of two per customer, but that didn't stop the hoarding onslaught fueled by fear! People would just leave one store and go to another until they had a stash and never gave a thought about sharing what was available with their fellow Americans. This meant "I got your back" was the first casualty in the epidemic.

China was known for having an abundant amount of viruses over the last fifteen hundred years, so I didn't pay too much attention to the news in late January 2020 about a new type of SARS virus in Wuhan, China. I was however quick to lift my head up from reading the paper one morning in February when Trump suggested on TV that there were five cases in the United States and this virus was not going to amount to anything.

I apologize, but whenever Trump says not to worry you can be sure there is something bad going to happen, and in just a few days there surely was something to worry about. Trump began playing down the disease and not wanting to see it emerge front and center on the news every day with the election only nine months away.

Two weeks passed, the virus broke out badly in nursing homes in Washington and California. The northeast was hit hard and NY Governor Cuomo blamed it on air travelers returning from Europe who unknowingly had been infected and had brought it back to the U.S. It was plain to see that the president was nervous and was only looking at how this virus was going to affect him in the upcoming election.

The CDC began stressing the need for everyone to maintain a safe distance (6 ft) from each other, wash your hands frequently, do not touch your face with your hands, and to wear masks that cover your nose and mouth. Trump railed at these suggestions as being excessive and would not wear a mask himself. This one stupid, arrogant, self-minded act would prove to be the underlying cause for the virus to spin out of control in the United States!

Meanwhile, unbeknownst to most Americans, 235 Americans boarded the Costa Luminosa cruise ship in Fort Lauderdale on March 5th and headed for Europe. At that time there were about 200 confirmed cases of the Covid virus in the United States. Word spread through the ship that three passengers who left the ship during port calls in the Caribbean tested positive for Covid; one died.

The State Department got involved and on Day 13 the cruise passengers learned they would be allowed off the ship in Marseille; France had just started a nationwide lockdown. The Americans had to gather in the ship's lounge to be checked by French medics before they were allowed to board buses for the airport. I do not remember seeing any of this on TV.

It was at this point when things became criminal because many of the passengers in their 70's had begun to show symptoms of the Covid virus and they were made to wait in the locked buses for five hours while paperwork was sorted out by U.S. diplomats.

It was midnight when they finally got on the jet hired by the cruise line. The flight back had all the ingredients of a super-spreader event. The airline advised the CDC of the arrival time of the plane loaded with infected passengers that was landing at Atlanta airport.

The jet took off for Atlanta at 2am and most of the passengers were relieved that the plane was landing in

Atlanta, headquarters of the CDC. The Atlanta airport is also one of 20 stations the CDC has around the U.S. to screen and quarantine ill travelers.

The passengers were told the CDC knew the plane was enroute into Atlanta, but didn't make plans to quarantine passengers when they arrived. Instead, the decision was made to treat them like any other Americans returning from Europe in March by having them fill out a health questionnaire. Can you believe this! This was a decision made at the top because Trump didn't want the media or anyone to hear about this plane load of infected Americans. About an hour before the plane touched down, the CDC's plan blew wide open. Remember earlier, when the French medics screened the passengers in the ship's lounge? It turns out the French tested four Americans for Covid, and three were positive and on the plane. That news went viral and surprised the CDC.

The entire saga was kept under wraps to protect the president. Criminal charges should be brought against him, the State Dept., the Justice Dept., and the CDC.

By March 20th, there were over 195,000 cases and almost 8,000 deaths worldwide. This was a new virus and the CDC did not have testing protocols in place that allowed for massive testing. The Trump administration was floundering as to what had to be done and Trump spent most of the time on TV not wearing a mask and playing down the severity of the pandemic and the need for testing and tracing. He was pushing back against testing and tracing because it was making the situation appear to look worse than he wanted it to look!

The U.S. found itself unprepared in the most basic of ways with respect to having an adequate supply of PPE (Personal Protection Equipment) for the healthcare sector and a serious shortage of ventilators. Emergency rooms across the nation started filling up with infected people and healthcare workers started dying at a faster rate because they did not have the proper PPE equipment or were re-using what they had over and over again.

President Trump was unable to step up to the plate and take hold of the pandemic as a leader, and when he did, he would proclaim some elixir, tonic, or disinfecting solution as a sure cure remedy for the virus. It wasn't long before the media began calling it Trump's traveling medicine show and his base remained super quiet because they too were concerned but not concerned to where they would stand up and challenge their president.

Trump announced that each state had to fend for themselves and this was in of itself his greatest failure as president for there was nowhere for the public to turn and states were low on funds. States began closing down restaurants, bars, schools, gyms, airports, ballparks, stadiums, churches, beaches, and before we knew it, 30 million people were out of work. Congress created a relief bill for $1.2T, the Senate passed it, the president signed it, and people across the land received $1200 relief checks.

Towards the middle of April, the curve for Covid-19 cases in the U.S began to flatten out a bit to where Trump's narcissism began to see this as an opportunity to regain his image and get his campaign back on track. In a flash, he took back control of the pandemic saying it's almost over and pressured the states to start re-opening businesses for the

Memorial Day weekend. At this juncture there were 760,000 cases and 40,000 deaths in the U.S.

Overnight, the states, especially the red states, began relaxing the safe distancing and mask requirements, beaches were reopened, and restaurants began to open. In just two weeks, the graphs spiked from 760K cases to 2.2 million cases and deaths doubled to 80 thousand bringing the total deaths in the U.S. to 120,000 people since the virus began. Fifty thousand cases and 1500 deaths were occurring every day in this country! Twenty five percent of all the cases in the world were in the USA. Some of Trump's supporters were to blame for this because they had more of an allegiance to Trump than they did to their common sense and wouldn't wear masks and safe distance. His supporters considered any media reports against their president to be fake news and would not accept Trump as being responsible for anything that was happening! Madness!

President Trump contracted the Covid virus and Congress decided to look into measures outlined in the 25th Amendment which allows Congress and/or the VP to take measures to insure the president was in fact operating with all his faculties because it's a must that we always have a leader whose thinking is not impaired in any way. Most importantly, it should not be a partisan issue which it soon became when Speaker Pelosi introduced the measure to Congress and the media. VP Pence remained silent.

The idea that the politicians of the same party as the president would want to block this move shows the degree of immaturity and obstinacy that prevails in the GOP party. Here we are in the middle of pandemic and Republican politicians put themselves, their party, and their future first and foremost. If you don't want to become a patsy you will need to remember which candidates are prone to this type of behavior to the best of your ability before you check the box. It's your <u>sacred</u> duty to make sure you are sending the most mature and level headed candidates from the very best of who we have to Washington DC; not the very worst! You need to ask them at a town hall meeting if they would in fact vote to activate the 25th Amendment if there was any doubt the president was not capable of fulfilling his duties because of any mental or physical issues.

It was not much different during the fall of 1918 when the Spanish Flu was raging in the U.S. Over 4500 people were dying a month in Philadelphia and the CDC blamed the 20 to 40 year old people for not taking the epidemic seriously. The Spanish Flu left 675,000 dead in the United States and most of the dead were due to Americans that would not comply with the CDC mask and self-quarantine suggestions.

Most of the supporters that showed up at a Trump re-election rally in Michigan in early September 2020 were not wearing face masks nor were they maintaining a safe distance from one another as advised by the CDC. A CNN crew interviewed several of them who began ridiculing the TV crew for wearing protective masks, and declared the Covid-19 pandemic was the greatest hoax of all time. Trump showed up without a mask giving further proof that he had their backs regarding them not needing to wear masks. Unbeknownst to many of his supporters though because they don't bother to read, Trump gets tested every day, especially after a rally which proves again why our founding fathers knew you could not put the future of this nation in the hands of folks who do not have the mental acuity to discern when they were a target of guile or being played by politicians, or as in this case, have dismissed their own survival instincts against a virus they say is a hoax when it's quite clear that it isn't. Has it always been this way? Maybe, but the pilgrims surely didn't behave this way! You can also bet that any Trump supporter that ended up in ICU wished that he or she had taken this virus more seriously.

The Covid virus is still raging across America. The virus has been going on for nine months and we are no further along in controlling it than we were at the onset. It became Trump's worst nightmare since he turned a blind eye to it in early February knowing full well its potency and what it could mean for him in the upcoming election. He chose not to do the next right thing which would have been to turn control of the disease over to the CDC and their world class epidemiologists and scientists, support their findings, and follow through with a nationwide virus policy. I have no doubt the virus would have been controlled until the scientists produced a vaccine for all of us, but that's not what happened and once again we the people have been played and left holding the bag.

Anthony Fauci made a misstatement about the same time in February when he was quoted as saying we don't need to wear face masks until the CDC says to and Trump used this misstep to show he himself was not guilty of any wrongdoing. Fauci corrected his misstatement asap and has since been on a mission asking every American to wear a mask and maintain a safe distance.

The CDC has the finest scientists, medical doctors, and epidemiologists in the world, and yet, they too have not lived up to their motto, 'Plan, Prepare, and Respond'. The CDC

Director, Robert Redfield, chose not to push back against the policies of the president knowing the president had no professional medical or scientific training when it comes to controlling a virus epidemic, and yet, he may have decided to acquiesce lest he be fired by the president; kind of reminds me of the TV game Trump hosted some years back called 'The Apprentice.'

Fauci is a member of the White House Covid-19 task Force and has been appearing on all the media networks since the onset of the virus espousing the need to wear face masks and maintaining safe distancing that has fallen on some deaf ears throughout the nation. I believe he would have done better had he resigned from the WH Covid-19 taskforce, and been a voice in the desert letting all of us know the truth without any trimmings. That's not what happened and it's plain to see that this may have taken a toll on him. I hope he would be the first to admit that Trump lacked the leadership qualities from the onset of this pandemic and We the People are at fault for not saying a word as well!

There is no doubt in my mind that disinformation and outright lies led to 8,408,340 Americans getting the disease that led to over 238,000 deaths with just 3 days to the election.

Just when you think nothing could be worse, Bob Woodward announced he had taped several interviews for his new book with the president since early February 2020 during which time the president said he knew the virus was going to be five times deadlier than a flu virus, and yet, he chose not to inform the public because it would have caused a panic. Another blatant lie! He did not tell the public because he was worried how this was going to affect his re-election period!

Where was the outburst from across America! Where was the blowback from his base, the Joint Chiefs of Staff, the troops, the GOP party for his outrageous remarks in France? Why are they kowtowing to this man! What happened to our sense of honor and decency!

An ex-WH aide told the press that there are people in the WH that believe this pandemic is a hoax and yet there are 13 staff members in the WH that tested positive for the virus, and the WH itself is trying to alter the Covid-19 infection data in order to get more schools re-opened; madness! No, it's criminal!

There was no sin or dereliction Trump could commit that would pressure his supporters to find fault with him even when some of what he did affected them, like the virus. It was like part of America has been under his spell for the last four years. I have come to see there are two totally different worlds of Trump supporters. The first world you will find those that are enamored with his illicit financial dealings, tawdry sexual behavior, and the vulgar demonization of his foes. The second world of Trumpers are those with skin in the money game!" They are the upper middleclass and elite Americans who have saved a fortune in taxes over the last four years in spite of the fact that it raised our nation's debt and I've not heard a shameful regret from one of them.

I reminded everyone I know not to forget what happened just twelve years ago after we elected our first black president who before he could take office inherited a country whose economy was all but left in the toilet by the previous Republican administration, and yet, he stood tall. He took measures to get us back on our feet, and was re-elected to continue the restoration of our economy which created over

250,000 jobs every month for the last two and a half years he was in office. He also managed to put most of the Wall Street investment bankers back in the box for pulling the rug out from under the world's economies.

I would like to add that Obama was not elected president of the United States because it was a good idea or it was time for us to have a black president; he was elected twice because he was the best of all of our best at that moment which is exactly what our founding fathers wanted and what Abraham Lincoln meant when he said, " … **It is for us the living, rather, to be dedicated here to the unfinished work which they who fought here have thus far so nobly advanced. It is rather for us to be here dedicated to the great task remaining before us…"**

This is also the right point in this narrative to let everyone know that Obama did in fact leave a Pandemic Response Plan for whoever would be the next president

Obama's White House National Security Council left the Trump administration a detailed document on how to respond to a pandemic. The document, whose existence was publicly revealed by Politico in March 2020, is called the Playbook for Early Response to High-Consequence Emerging Infectious Disease Threats and Biological Incidents.

Ben Rhodes, who served as deputy national security adviser to Obama, said on Twitter in response to McConnell's disclaimer, "The maddening thing is Obama left them a literal playbook, a cabinet-level exercise, and a global infrastructure to deal with 'something like this,'"

Ron Klain, a Democratic campaign adviser to Joe Biden and former administration Ebola response coordinator wrote on Twitter, "We literally left them a 69-page Pandemic Playbook ... they chose to ignore it,"

The playbook — 40 pages plus appendices — contains step-by-step advice on questions to ask, decisions to make, and which federal agencies are responsible for what. It includes sample documents that officials could use for inter-agency meetings. And it explicitly lists novel coronaviruses as one of the kinds of pathogens that could require a major response.

The color-coded, checklist-style document addresses issues like testing, funding, personal protective equipment, emergency declarations, border control measures, diplomacy, the use of the military, public communication, even mortuary services.

It lays out dozens of key questions to ask at certain stages of the response like "Should there be arrangements for medivac or in-country clinical care advisory for U.S. Persons?" ... "What is the robustness of contact tracing?" ... "Is the incident likely to impact housing such that alternative housing needs may become necessary?" It outlined key decisions to determine whether to implement screening and monitoring measures, or other travel measures within the US or globally; prioritization and allocation of resources subject to the Defense Production Act; "How to tailor waste management plans to incident specific conditions".

"While each emerging infectious disease threat will present itself in a unique way, a consistent, capabilities-based approach to addressing these threats will allow for faster decisions with more targeted expert subject matter input from federal departments and agencies." The document says all of this.

There could be valid criticisms of Obama's pandemic preparations, and it's possible to argue that the playbook was inadequate for the current pandemic. A current Trump appointed NSC official, whom Politico quoted anonymously, described the 2016 document as "quite dated." It's not clear who in the Trump administration saw the 69-page playbook, but I certainly wouldn't want it known if I said it was "quite dated". Maybe the FBI should go down every rabbit hole in Washington to find out.

In addition to the playbook, outgoing senior Obama officials also led an in-person pandemic response exercise for senior incoming Trump officials in January 2017 — as required by a new law on improving presidential transitions that Obama signed in 2016. Politico reported in March that the meeting, attended by current Trump Cabinet officials including Energy Secretary Rick Perry and Transportation Secretary Elaine Chao, addressed how to deal with a hypothetical flu crisis, among other scenarios.

So, it's clearly untrue that Obama left no 'game plan' at all and even if he hadn't that doesn't absolve Trump and his do-nothing administration from hitting the dirt running and coming up with their own plan which they didn't do. Truth is, Trump trusted no one and abhorred anything that had to do with Obama and would never have adopted a plan from Obama even if it was signed off by Jesus Christ Himself!

Over the next six months, the virus killed 190,000 Americans who were mostly the elderly and healthcare workers working on the front lines in hospitals across the nation. 30 million Americans have been laid off.

The virus is in its 9th month with no clear response over the disease in sight. The WH continues to manipulate the data with which to persuade the governors and public of each state to start opening up their schools and businesses regardless of what the positivity rates indicate or what is not the best way going forward. It's clearly all about Trump wanting to remain the king of America!

Trump appointed Scott Atlas, a neuroradiologist to his Covid response team. Scott favored developing a plan like that of Sweden which by the way is a near disaster. Herd immunity is a spin off from the Darwinist theory that supposes the herd will be stronger if you let the disease go through the herd; survival of the fittest!

Schools across the country are opening and re-closing due to spikes in the virus. Over 9 million Americans were infected by October 31, 2020 and here it is five weeks later and that number is now at 13 million infected cases and over 260,000 deaths. Forty states are about to go into another lockdown and most Americans remain on self-imposed isolation. Two million Americans opted to travel by air over Thanksgiving after the CDC practically begged them not to. The young people continue to engage in groups without practicing recommended safe distances or wearing masks. But that too is taking its toll in ways that may have finally gotten their attention. It seems there are long lasting medical conditions that linger on long after the disease goes away …oops … their self-absorbed myopic view of the world through their favorite media didn't see that one coming! As for the president's take, he proclaimed last week that he isn't to blame for any of the Covid problems.

So, there you have it. The question becomes, how would Trump supporters come to the conclusion that Trump did indeed look out for their welfare and best interests by the way he handled the Covid-19 virus? His only fear from the time he learned of the virus was how was this going to affect him election day; not how will I bring the finest epidemiological minds, scientists, and officials together to develop and implement strategies to save as many Americans as possible.

Again, we keep coming back to the same question, what does all of this have to do with who should or should not have the right to vote? Evidently, there is no question that the Founders did believe in the higher good when it came to who was going to be allowed to vote, otherwise they would've just let everyone vote, but for sure, they did not think everyone had the spiritual or mental acuity to cast a ballot with so much at stake. I can only imagine which Americans they would or wouldn't let vote today.

Trump hung the nation out to dry from the moment he was alerted of the virus. He down played the use of masks and distancing and chose to focus on how the virus could hurt the economy which in turn would hurt his chances to get re-elected.

Most Americans remember what happened when Senator Edward Kennedy's car veered off the bridge at Chappaquiddick Island near Edgartown on Martha's Vineyard Island during the night of July 18, 1969 resulting in the death of 28 year old Mary Jo Kopechne. Ted Kennedy managed to escape the vehicle, swim to the shore, but did not report what happened to the authorities for 10 hours.

Kennedy would proclaim over and over that he had tried several times to swim back to the car to save Mary Jo but the rapid tidal flow pulled him away from the scene. When the car was pulled from the water the trunk was dry which meant Mary Jo didn't drown, but died a slow death of suffocation. It was ruled an accident and Kennedy was not cited; eleven years later he pondered running for the office of the president.

The reason I am writing about this is twofold. I found his decision to run for president lacking any sensibility or respect for the Office of the Presidency or his constituents, especially when you consider how he behaved that night before the accident when there may have been excessive drinking at the cottage and moral concern when he and Mary Jo decided to leave in the car together. He spent ten hours following the accident getting all his ducks in a row.

So, when Ted Kennedy announced that he might run for president, many folks in and outside of Washington DC took a dim view of this because of how he behaved the night of the accident and the following day when he looked like he was having difficulty getting his story straight. This backlash must have had an effect on Ted for he decided not to run in that election, but he did end up being re-elected Senator several times that made the people of Massachusetts and the rest of the country proud of him.

This is exactly how our founders hoped We the People would protect the Office of the President from those who had few to no scruples or principles. There is no doubt in my mind that I wouldn't have handled the aftermath of the accident much different than Ted Kennedy did leaving me no doubts that I too should not have been eligible to hold any office in the land if I had behaved in a similar fashion. If Ted Kennedy had saved Mary Jo that night the nation might've proclaimed him a hero, but would that confirm he had the moral character to be the president; I don't think so.

The question you all have to ask yourselves is, "Would this have been the case with Mr. Trump? I don't think so as well. Truth, decency, and honor became the first casualties after Trump became a candidate in the GOP primary for president. The nightly news became a nonstop sewer of events that would rattle the moral fiber of the best Americans and maybe a few underworld figures as well. Families had to shoo their younger children out of the den when Trump was out on the campaign trail making vulgar and lewd comments never before heard on TV from a presidential candidate.

We all know where it went from there, but what you may not know is how this president adversely affected some of our younger generation of school age children. What are some of his supporters telling their children after their children queried their parents about this president's lies and his behavior with woman? What kind of a broad brush stroke did some parents use to glaze over the truth in defense of Trump? 'Oh, he was only kidding' or 'Oh, he's stretching the truth to make a point', because if this is what they did, they have probably given their children's moral compass a sufficient enough twist to last them two lifetimes. How are these children supposed to navigate the field of honor and decency if their parents have glazed over all of this immoral behavior or worse, don't even care?

With the exception of those that voted for Trump, we the general public have become numb and somewhat passive when he spews out lie after lie during his briefings with reporters behind the WH every day for the last four years; over 22,000 lies and that in itself is beyond the pale. His own sister and niece have painted him as having a troubled sociopathic and narcissistic personality, and yet, his base doesn't want to hear any of this "fake news!" I can somewhat understand why they said the hell with it and voted for him in 2016, but what are they now thinking after they have seen him in real life for the last four years?

They surely cannot be that naive or numb to know that he doesn't care about their well-being or safety especially with respect to this virus. Maybe some of his supporters have the same filter he has that prevents them from seeing that he has no moral fiber … no scruples … no principles … no respect for our fallen soldiers when he refers to them as losers and suckers … no respect for the world scientists when he pulled the U.S. out of the Paris Accords … no sense of endangering the public when he lied about the extent of the Covid virus when he knew otherwise ... idolizing authoritarian and autocratic leaders around the world … him having the same dark motives when he promotes white supremacy and racism as did his grandfather who marched in the KKK parade in NYC in 1914 … has no sense of duty, honor, country when he accepts the word of Putin our foremost adversary ... doesn't allow any note taking when they met for two hours at Helsinki … has absolutely no empathy or sense of decency for having instructed the U.S. Border Patrol to extract the children from their parents and then shipped them all over our country to where most of them will never see their parents again … sided with Saudi Prince Mohammed Bin

Salman over the killing of Jamal Khashoggi after most of the world's intelligence services confirmed the Prince ordered the killing … cannot utter a complete sentence without turning the truth into a preposterous fabrication … non-stop demonizing of anyone he perceives as a threat on Twitter … a confirmed sexual predator who brags about his sexual conquests over gorgeous woman … gave a tax cut to the top one percenters which now allows some of them to pay an 8.5% adjusted income tax or no tax at all … was seen several times in photos taken with Jeffrey Epstein, a rich financier who was an accused sexual predator of teenage girls who mysteriously died in a NYC federal lockup while he awaited his trial. … has no qualms about using his Office of the Presidency to promote business opportunities for his family and his world-wide companies. No, I do not understand how his base can support someone like him let alone vote for him and I hope some of the children of his supporters don't as well..

Abraham Maslow may have put it correctly when he said, "The management assumes no responsibility for what is found", for it aptly seems to fit what has been going on with me and some of us; I want to blame somebody but that will catapult me into the role of a victim; I hate being a victim! Abraham is suggesting that if I can accept the difficult message that my feelings are mine to deal with and no one else's, acceptance and self-improvement begins; I hope so.

In the movie Forest Gump, his mother gave Forest many one-liners that were full of wisdom that she hoped would carry him through the tough times of his life. One such line was, "Stupid is what stupid does." It seems to fit what's been going on here and around the world over the last four years with respect to countries that were flourishing democracies like Hungary and Poland that are now leaning toward autocratic rule supported by other authoritarian rulers like Russia, China, Iran, North Korea, Philippines, Myanmar, and many others.

Because I am the writer, I'm going to use this opportunity to mention something of an irritation in my community. We have a post office in my community that is situated in a good location, has a large parking lot, plenty of personal mail boxes inside, and several employees to wait on the customers. There was also a drive through lane out front with an outside mailbox that had been there since this post office was built that everyone loved, especially when it was raining. About seven years ago the drive by mailbox was stolen one night and it has not been replaced since. These are the things that really get under peoples skin. I've queried different employees at the counter several times hoping they were going to replace it and I continually get the shrug of the shoulders, in other words, this case is closed. Having a drive through mailbox was wonderful for the thousands of seniors in the area and would have kept us much safer during the Covid epidemic, but because we have some short sighted, self-serving, bureaucratic officials and managers working in our U.S. Postal Office system, everyone has had to go into the building for last seven years and this last year of the Covid virus to send their mail. Woefully inconsiderate!

The meaning of the word addiction in the dictionary; a compulsive, chronic, physiological or psychological need for a habit-forming substance, behavior, or activity having harmful physical, psychological, or social effects and typically causing well-defined symptoms (such as anxiety, irritability, tremors, or nausea) upon withdrawal or abstinence; the state of being addicted. Can folks be addicted to leaders; they were with Hitler!

Politicians for the most part have always been stirring up the populace to get themselves elected to where we now find ourselves doing the stirring amongst ourselves. We have switched places with our leaders and become divisive, nasty, pointed, and disrespectful with each other, and of course, no one is willing to see their part in any of this.

Chapter 14

The first presidential debate took place a week ago which was a little over a month before the election and most networks described it as a train wreck. Trump was a bully and kept interrupting Joe Biden to where both of them began to speak over each other and had a difficult time staying on topic or delivering a message. The moderator asked President Trump if he would denounce the white supremacy movement and it took him several minutes to finally blurt out. "I will, I will … I'll tell them to stand down and standby!" Not a pretty picture of an American president, and for sure not how Trump wanted it to turn out with him being 10 points behind in the polls and not gaining any ground.

The Covid pandemic made it all but impossible for an in person third debate and Trump decided he didn't want any part of a virtual debate and opted to continue trying to feel good going maskless to his rallies. His inability to see that this reckless message was killing people may have been the main reason for him being behind in the polls, although his inability to trust anyone in his cabinet or the world for that matter has been his crowning failure during his presidency.

It still is not known if Trump would have tested positive the day of the second debate, although he did test positive two days later and was taken by Marine One helicopter to Walter Reed hospital the following day where he received special medication cocktails and steroid injections. Sunday, he left the hospital for an hour to take a ride in a bullet proof Suburban waving to onlookers around the area. Sad to think he'd put the Secret Service personnel in harm's way to get a photo-op to prove he was doing well. He received a Covid vaccination as well and did not want the public informed, especially his supporters.; talk about the epitome of him playing his supporters.

The polling places will start to close across the country in about three hours. I have never seen an election like this one; anxiety would be an understatement.

A newsperson was interviewing a voter coming out of a poll, "How do you feel?" … "I feel exhausted and yet I am so relieved I voted. I am angry that some Americans will not be able to cast their vote due to voter suppression which is why it's so important for the rest of us to vote and change the laws so this does not continue to happen in our country; it's our sacred right and duty and the only way we the people can rectify injustice is in the ballot box. The founders knew what they were doing!" The GOP has increased voter repression, especially in the South and the upper mid-west over the last 25 years. It's illegal and the officials should be charged by the AG!

Trump just finished an interview with the press wherein he admitted aloud that he hates losing, "I'm a very poor loser." I believe he might very well might have won the election if he had delivered on what he promised to do during his first term and let the CDC experts manage the pandemic. He promised not to lower taxes on the rich and ended up giving them a tax cut . He said he was going to launch a mega billion dollar infrastructure program that never got started. He promised to repeal Obamacare and thank God that never happened! He promised to build a wall on the Mexico border and Mexico was going to pay for it; only 300 miles of the wall was completed and Mexico didn't pay for any of it.

Here it is the day after the election and Trump is in the lead by less than a point with no clear winner. I sat on the patio disappointed but acquiescing to the process knowing whatever happens will be the will of the people.

On Day 3, Minnesota, Wisconsin, and Michigan all went to Biden which I felt was a miracle that left Biden ahead with 253 electoral votes to Trump's 214. Biden maintained a slight edge over Trump all week in Arizona, Nevada, Pennsylvania, and Georgia after most of the in person votes had been counted. The counting of the mail in ballots favored Biden 2 to 1. Trump was not having any success in the courts trying to stop the counting of the mail in ballots in Pennsylvania. GOP senators from Pennsylvania declared there was no wrongdoing in the ballot counting. Trump attacked the outcome of the vote in Michigan going to Biden claiming it was rigged! Funny how he never once thought the 2016 election that he won was rigged; but it was and in his favor!

We Americans owe the Republican governors, secretaries of states, poll workers, and supervisors of elections in all the 50 states our gratitude for remaining steadfast under the Trump onslaught to throw out votes and declare the election a fraud; this was America at its finest and Trump at his worst!

Biden held off making any announcements that he was the winner and Trump voiced that he was not going to concede.

Governor DeSantis started riling the Trump base up in Florida to contact their Senators which was nothing but a spoiler's attempt to exacerbate what was already an explosive situation and him wanting to remain in Trump's favor! Shame on him! Over 110,000 Covid cases a day have emerged across the U.S. for the last three days with no letup in sight. Shame on them all!

Joint Chiefs of Staff Chairman Gen. Mark Milley announced to the press yesterday, "We are unique among militaries, we do not take an oath to a king or a queen, a tyrant, or a dictator. We do not take an oath to any individual. We do take an oath to the Constitution." Talk about words pointing directly at Trump and welcomed words for us Americans during these unsettled times when the standing president is doing every thing within his power to declare war on Iran and declare the election a fraud. He still will not concede and wants to remain the king. Thank you General Milley!

On Day 5, Biden made his victory speech from Wilmington, Delaware that was welcomed around the world! If he does nothing over the next four years but stop the nasty negative rhetoric coming from the White House, create a neutral zone for us to lower our guard, and help to lower the temperature in Washington DC to where each of us can stop being so contentious, then he will have done wonders.

PBS aired a documentary this week called Nazis Rise to Power and I got the chills watching it. The similarities between what has been going on since Trump got elected president and how Hitler came to power are damn near identical! General Schleicher had the ear of Chancellor Hindenburg from 1930 to 1933 and was himself using and abusing his power to ultimately gain control of all power in Germany. He wasn't as clever as Adolph Hitler though when it came to knowing how to use storm troopers to instill fear in his opponents, break up communist protests that were gaining strength, and intimidate the citizens throughout Germany that didn't have a clue as to what or who was on the horizon. For three years Hitler had the political, fascist, and autocratic savvy to twist every truth and incident into a lie that benefitted him and outwitted his opponents. The German people never knew what happened until it was too late for anyone to stop him and Germany was all but handed to him on a silver platter three years later. Ring any bells … because if you cannot connect the dots of what took place in Germany to what has just taken place in the U.S. over the last four years, then you have not been paying attention or you've knowingly or unknowingly been swallowing all of Trump's political diatribes hook, line, and sinker.

We have been given a breather and we best open our eyes and see what has just taken place although it's going to be difficult for some of us to do … remember, no one likes to admit that they've been had!

In the meantime, Trump's lawyers have failed in 53 attempts to get a favorable ruling in any federal or state court to overturn the results of the election in Michigan and Pennsylvania. Trump's base continues to protest in some cities for what they believe was a rigged election and they are making plans to re-elect Trump in the 2024 election. Trump boasts he was a street kid in the Queens, but I'll bet he forgot street kids don't like poor losers. You can also bet Trump would not be permitted to run in 2024 if he had to submit to an MMPI (Minnesota Multiphasic Personal Inventory) test.

The New York Times just released a story that Trump was depositing all his ongoing campaign donations in a Delaware LLC account. The Delaware law for this type of LLC account allows Trump to use these funds any way he sees fit; NYT estimates he has $500 million leftover out of $1.3

billion campaign donations plus $250 million he has received since the end of the election. Sure hope the IRS and DOJ are paying attention because this is beyond being ludicrous!

Trump is beginning to see that he has no chance of winning the election via the courts, but that hasn't stopped his vindictiveness to where he began gutting the government in ways never before thought possible and the GOP is just watching it all as if there was nothing they could do or worse, wanted to do.

Trump closed down the U.S. involvement in the Open Skies Treaty and ordered the two C-135 aircraft used in this treaty sent to the junkyard. This treaty allowed Russian surveillance aircraft to fly over the U.S. to ensure the U.S. wasn't constructing more missile silos. You cannot imagine how this pleased Putin because now we cannot fly over Russia as well. How strange that of all the things he could dismantle he chose this one! America sits mute while this six year old boy who no longer is going to be allowed to play king in the White House is gutting the Pentagon.

The moment that everyone has been waiting for arrived; the pardons. Unlike the pardoning of the WH turkey named Peas before Thanksgiving, some of these pardons are going to be closer to Trump; like George Papadopoulos, his former campaign worker who was found guilty of lying to the FBI; former congressmen Duncan Hunter and Chris Collins who were convicted of financial crimes; four former Blackwater contractors for their part in the killing of Iraqi civilians at a Baghdad intersection in broad daylight; Paul Manafort was sentenced to seven years for a variety of federal crimes related to the Trump campaign and Russian operatives;

Roger Stone convicted of witness tampering, lying to the FBI, and obstructing congressional investigation into Trump campaign collusion with Russia; and Charles Kushner, father of Jarod Kushner for 18 counts of income tax evasion in 2005.

It's expected that before he leaves the WH he is going to submit pardons for all his family that worked or lived in the White House.

There's two more days left in the year and folks cannot wait for the year to be over. I don't know which is worse; the virus or the president who is still doing everything within his power to throw out the election results in several states; he's become a scary despot!

People are dying worldwide at the rate 15,000 a day and 3500 a day in the United States. Europe reached 500,000 deaths since the outbreak of the virus with no sign of letting up.

The Trump Administration promised to have 20 million Americans vaccinated before the end of the year; only 2.1 million will be vaccinated. The virus has mutated into more potent variants over the last few weeks which is not good news; some of the first cases with the new strains are showing up in the U.S.

Covid virus hospitalizations have placed many hospitals at full capacity again with some running 15-25 percent over capacity. Healthcare staff in the U.S. are over worked to where some of them are reaching their limits.

Congress enacted a Covid relief bill just days before the end of 2020, the main purpose of which was supposed to extend unemployment protection for another 50 weeks ($120 billion) and keep the government open. Included in this bill was a stimulus package that gave $600 to those making up to $75,000 a year and $1200 for those making up to $150,000 a year ($166 billion), forgivable loans to business owners ($284 billion), $160 billion to schools and universities, and an assortment of assistance to other agencies that bring the total of the bill to $1.4 trillion. This means that all of the above added up to about $570 billion and the rest of the government agencies will receive $830 billion. This is where it becomes important for everyone to read the bill. As an afterthought, President Trump wants everyone to get a $2000 check! He wants to be remembered in a generous light. Hopefully, those that don't need it will pass it on to those that do.

The GOP and Trump are quick to offer financial assistance to those affected by the Covid virus, but they did nothing in the way of enacting emergency measures that would prevent the spread of the disease. The disease started in China and yet China only experienced 5,000 deaths. This is because China created laws forbidding people to go out into public without a mask. The Chinese were free to do anything the wanted to do during the epidemic except not wear a mask or ignore social distancing rules.

Governor De Santis of Florida who always will do anything to remain in a favorable light with Trump, just submitted a bill to the Florida Senate forbidding businesses to require patrons to have Covid Vaccination cards in order to enter their establishments. So, let me see if I have this right. When Scotus ruled in favor of the Christian baker in Colorado who refused to bake a wedding cake for a gay couple, this was okay. But it's not okay to enact laws that will prevent

Americans from infecting other Americans with a life threatening disease?

The words from the Canadian stewardess who asked the passenger to leave the plane because he smelled terribly came front and center; "You Yanks are so free that you are going to keep on trespassing over each other's boundaries until someone gets hurt."

Chapter 15

Every year, personnel working inside nuclear facilities must undergo an MMPI (Minnesota Multi-Phasic Personality) test in order to determine if they have aberrant tendencies and if anyone tests positive for these tendencies they would not be permitted to work in any nuclear facility. This test was also used by different departments of the government to screen applicants for the intelligence sector, FBI, CIA, NSA, police departments, military, etc.

This test can also determine if people are of a sound mind and do not have depression, hysteria, psychopathic issues, paranoia, psychasthenia, schizophrenia, social introversion, or any aberrant tendencies that would cause a person to harm others or sabotage equipment at a nuclear facility.

I am of an opinion that this test should be taken by everyone; candidates running for local, state, or federal office, especially candidates running for the office of presidency, the president's entire cabinet, all people in the armed services, judicial positions, all law enforcement personnel, all employees in the local, state, and federal justice departments, all government employees, when applying for an automobile drivers license, cruise ship captains and mates, and all airline pilots and FAA personnel for starters.

I also believe this test should be taken by all students starting with the 5th grade to determine if the student has bullied other students or has been bullied or exposed to malicious media attacks by other students.

There are almost 500 questions and the test can take three to four hours to complete although I would think there are shorter or abbreviated versions that are used to raise a red flag. About seven percent of all people that take the test to work in nuclear facilities fail the test and therefore would not be allowed to work inside a nuclear facility which means they would not be able to provide for their family.

So, why should workers at nuclear facilities have to take the test and possibly fail when candidates for high offices and other high risk positions are not obliged to take the test. Do we suppose the mental health of our elected leaders is above those that work in nuclear facilities? I would hope not, but just look at how some of our leaders have behaved. Why would we not want to make sure our president who has access to the black box has excellent mental health? You can be sure there'll be push back from both sides of the aisles in both houses if they were obliged to take this test for fear they may have an even higher failure rate.

The WHO (World Health Organization) proclaimed several years ago that forty percent of all Americans have some degree of mental health challenges that would lead to some degree of poor mental health. This means one of every three Americans is not quite right when it comes to having good mental health!

The MMPI test is the perfect tool for us to use to put a stop to us sending self-serving, mentally deficient and somewhat disingenuous leaders to Washington that have only one mission; maintain a hold on their office, maintain an environment for folks just like themselves, and zig-zag through the constitutional road blocks to advance their personal agendas.

Some of this is genetic and some has transpired with societal issues and the introduction of the personal computer and smart phones that are making us all the more sophisticated and self-absorbed than we already were. We are fast becoming the alpha-omega of our own existence in the unhealthiest of ways which can only lead to a loss of spiritual and psychological well-being as well. Remember, 70 years ago almost every kid dropped their school books in the house and went out to play every day after school; that's not the case today.

I believe that individuals that know they have mental challenges that are faced with having to take an MMPI test may seek professional help, especially if these challenges would prevent them from achieving their life's goals which would be good for them and us as a nation. The test may even raise some red flags for those individuals that will be prone to the use and abuse of drugs and alcohol! We will not survive by ignoring the elephants in the rooms. I agree with the NRA that it's not the gun that should be outlawed, but I do believe that all citizens should not be able to purchase or have access to a gun unless they pass an MMPI test.

Nor should a person be able to operate a motor vehicle, fly a plane, command a warship, have access to explosives, teach or oversee our children, have access to the black box, or apply for any position in our country that could put the welfare of the public in harm's way unless they have passed an MMPI test.

With respect to different visions for the future, we need only recall what was going in the world in George Orwell's book, 1984, to get a view of what might lie ahead. This dystopian science fiction novel imagines a future in a totalitarian state of Britain now called Airstrip One. The world had suffered a series of nuclear wars that left mega-lunatic leaders in charge of what and who remained; mental illness and deprivation prevailed to make matters worse. I saw the movie in 1954 and here it is now 66 years later that I am beginning to understand how this could have happened. It begins with nations breaking up into mentally unhealthy groups with each group suspecting the other groups of undermining what's left of reality to where no one trusts anyone.

Only healthy societies can prevent nations from falling into the "we know best" trap. Just because Russians have the right to vote don't think for a minute that the average Russian voters believe their vote will get counted and if that doesn't wake you up you needn't read on any further.

I keep trying to bring everyone back to the founders and asking who would they allow to vote because they genuinely knew the human condition better than our leaders do today. Just because I have reached a certain voting age does not mean that I have the mature and spiritual embodiments that make up good reasoning.

I am convinced every American should have to undergo an abbreviated MMPI and spiritual acuity test along with an American History test to determine if he or she should be allowed to vote; immigrants have to pass a history test in order to receive their American citizenship which means they had to study our history before taking the test!

More importantly, what could be wrong with each of us submitting to a mental evaluation and a look see at our moral compasses? God knows some us could use a good brain washing! And for sure, most Americans couldn't even pass the test that the immigrants take to become a citizen. Why would brushing up on American history in order pass a test to vote and re-commit ourselves to the re-dedication of the unfinished work that those at Gettysburg so nobly began be such a bad thing? We have to study to take a test to get a driver's license ... which is more important?

Chapter 16

We've been passive about learning how to get along with each other for the last 100,000 years; goodness and good things take time and have to be practiced if they're going to be appreciated. It also appears that white people do not do well when they are in situations not of their choosing, like forced integration or being out voted by people of color, but if they can submit wonders do occur.

A ship carrying the first slaves to the New World arrived immediately after the arrival of the first 700 colonialists at Point Comfort which is now known as Hampton Roads, Virginia in 1619. It would seem that the very first white colonialists that came to America had planned on making their fortunes using slaves for no sooner had they arrived here ships carrying slaves from Africa arrived soon after. There were 4 million slaves by 1860.

It is also somewhat incomprehensible to believe that the common Christian folks that arrived in Virginia in 1619 didn't think there was anything spiritually or morally wrong with one human being buying another human being for their own personal use. Surely, they had to have pondered or considered that these slaves were no longer going to have dominion over their own lives, never receive any monetary compensation whatsoever for their labor, would have their offspring taken from them and sold for profit, and would be punished or whipped for the slightest acts of insubordination or breaking of the owner's rules. The slave owners were wily and protected themselves in a cloak of innocence by maintaining the Negro people were slightly advanced offspring from monkeys, but surely they were not humans.

I'll bet there were few white people in the South that believed this to be the case.

The Civil War broke out between the North and the South in 1861; the North wanted to abolish slavery and the South wanted no part of that although to this day some folks from the South will argue the facts of history and suggest they entered the war because of Yankee aggression forgetting the South fired the first shots when they attacked Fort Sumpter on April 12, 1861. On September 22, 1862, President Lincoln issued the Proclamation Emancipation freeing the slaves. This was year into the war and had no immediate effect on the freeing of the slaves but it did embolden the southern locals and slave owners to mock the slaves and treat them with even less dignity if that was possible. The South surrendered on April 9, 1965 which ended hostilities. On June 19, 1865 slaves began to be freed in the south. The economy of the South had all but been obliterated. The South which was now under the boot of the Jim Crow movement denied any hospitality to the carpetbaggers and rejected any form of reconstruction assistance from the North.

Here we are 150 years after the Civil War and many of the white folks in the USA still do not accept let alone welcome the black ancestors of the slaves into their communities. Racialism is unfinished spiritual business that leaves those afflicted with it in a constant state of upheaval, separation, and pain. All of what is taking place today is what was left unfinished 150 years ago. The white citizens in the South turned a blind eye to their inhumanity and accepted their share of the trickle down profits from slavery. To assuage their consciences they agreed with the plantation owners that the slaves were nothing more than inferior black creatures from Africa. This was a dichotomy for if they truly believed this was the case, why did most southern states imprison and levy heavy fines on anyone found teaching a black slave how to read? Inferior beings or non-humans could not possibly learn how to read. The slave owners and white citizens knew from the beginning what they were doing wasn't right.

There was no way that the whites would ever have sat down with the freed slaves after the Civil War ended and discussed their part in all that had taken place over the previous 200 years; things may have been different if they had, but that didn't happen!

We were created in such a way that we cannot separate ourselves from those we are mistreating or holding down which is why all whites, north and south, must come together and agree that some of their ancestors committed grave atrocities against the black Africans.

The whites were unable to put the blacks out of sight and out of mind which is the reason why the Jim Crow era came into existence; guilt just doesn't go away. It was one thing to see black slaves loading supplies into a wagon in town with a slave master holding a whip before the Civil War ended, and it was another thing to see them coming and going as equal citizens. It was just too painful for the whites to accept for they each knew deep down they had played a part in this atrocity that had begun so long, long ago.

The Ku Klux Klan was formed and its members began dragging blacks from their homes in the middle of the night and lynching them. They burned down entire black villages throughout the south over the next 50 years hoping this would frighten them into leaving the South. They overlooked the fact that almost all of the slaves in 1865 had been born in the South and this was the only home they'd ever known; they weren't going anywhere! Why should they; they were born Americans!

The question in my mind is not so much what happened as why did it happen; why did the southerners persecute the Negros who had been slaves? Why did they not have some degree of empathy knowing these poor souls had been kidnapped, brought to America in the holds of ships like cattle for 244 years, worked for nothing, suffered beatings by the slave masters, and had their offspring taken from them and sold into slavery.

Why! Racism, racialism, xenophobia, colonialism, apartheid, genocide are all means of one group of people gaining superiority over others of different colors and ethnicities for societal and financial gain. This behavior begs every white supremist or racist to ask or at least ponder all of this because all of what I have been writing about is of a spiritual nature and all spiritual issues are paradoxical which means in this case, those afflicted with racism have switched places with the slaves.

Our Creator made us spiritually reciprocal to ensure a part of us would have to remain connected with those that we hated, denigrated, or persecuted. What's worse, we cannot throw a switch to change this or legislate laws that force us to be kind and loving because it's an inside job. Nor is punishing those with this adversity going to remedy this character defect. We the People have to forgive them, love them, hug them, and pray that they will receive nothing but goodness for the rest of their lives; it's what the Master would want us to do! In other words, it's not their fault! Generations were raised or influenced in a likewise manner by those that also had done this unto others; so on and so forth!

Remember the scene in Les Miserables when the gendarmes dragged the thief with a bag of silverware back to the bishop's rectory, " Here is your silver and this is the man we caught that had it" ... "Oh no, there must be some mistake ... this silver was a gift to him." Jean Valjean was a thief and this simple act of kindness changed him to where he learned how to love and appreciate his fellow man. He became a protagonist and a leader in the French revolution.

George Ritchie wrote a true story called Return from Tomorrow wherein he mentions an incident that was discovered when our troops first came upon a Nazi death camp in Germany. The degree in which the German guards treated the Jewish prisoners was beyond unmerciless to where some of our troops became sick and incapacitated. Ritchie came upon one of the prisoners in this death camp who didn't look like the others and surmised that he couldn't have been there long. He wasn't emaciated, he walked erectly, and he had an air of peace about him. They named him Wild Bill Cody because of his drooping handlebar mustache and his Polish name was too hard to pronounce. He helped the troops sort out many questions about what had taken place there. Further discussions with him revealed somethings of even more importance. This man said, "Only after I had been at the camp for a number of weeks did I realize what a rarity it was to see so many different nationalities of prisoners that hated each other as much as they hated the Germans."

He went on, "My family lived in the Jewish section of Warsaw." He began to get teary eyed, "My wife, two daughters, and three little boys were lined up against a wall with the other Jews in the neighborhood and the German guards opened up with their machine guns. I had begged them to let me die with them. I knew I had to decide right then and there whether to let myself hate or forgive the soldiers. It was an easy decision; I was a lawyer and I had already seen too many people that hated each other. Hate just killed six people who mattered most to me in the world. I decided then I would spend the rest of my life ... whether it was a few days or many days ... loving every person I came in contact with." That was in 1939 and he had been in the death camp for 6 years.

Every year since the end of the Civil War southerners continue to come together in droves to celebrate Civil War battle reenactments. They relived some of the epic battles that took place throughout the south which seems to lift or redeem their spirits. They also retell their version of what led to the war and how it ended because this was what was passed down to each generation since the war ended. The people in the south were disappointed when they lost, they became angry, vengeful, and the Negros happened to be the ones close at hand for them to blame and terrify. It's been 156 years and some southerners still are unable to offer a simple apology to the descendants of the slaves. Shame hurts deeply!

The Blacks I know have put the shamed ones into the hands of God.

To this day, most whites still haven't come to terms with their ancestor's part in all of these tragedies because racism is a blight in the soul and too painful to admit.

I had the opportunity to work in Calabar, Nigeria in 1967. Calabar was a city of 100,000 black Ebos and maybe a few hundred whites. Nigeria had won its independence from Great Britain in 1964 and a civil war was getting ready to break out between the Housas which were the ruling Muslim tribe in the Northwest and the Ebos which were a predominantly Christian tribe in the Southeast.

I never was disrespected by any of the Ebos, in fact, I have to this day never received such warmth, cordiality and friendship from blacks anywhere in the world as I did from these people. I was even invited to an all-black pre-war rally a few weeks before hostilities broke out and introduced to their leaders. This was not however how the Ebos felt about the Brits that still lived there after having been under their boots for centuries; there were still a lot of hard feelings from the way the Brits treated these people and they could see the difference from the way some of us Yanks were treating them with utmost respect that it was an inside job! You cannot fake it … it's either real or not real!

Patrick, my cook, awoke me at 11p one evening, "Master, you must get up and get dressed. My friend who works at the airport called and told me that the airport is being closed and the last airplane will be leaving in 45 minutes." Patrick lived on the other side of town and had called Thomas my driver to drive him to my apartment. They helped me pack my things in a suitcase and drove me to the airport in time for me to catch a flight to Lagos. The war broke out and I but for the Grace of God and Patrick did make it safely back home to the states. Two million Ebos died in this war and I too may have been one of them if it wasn't for Patrick. I saw no other white men boarding the plane that night.

I took these memories home with me 50 years ago and let them guide me in all my relationships with people of color and there is no question that every person of color that I have met knew that I truly accepted them as an equal and respected them, and for this I have been repaid a thousand times over throughout my life; and yes, it's an inside job.

My skin is white and I had nothing to say about it. Some white folks sincerely believe that them having white skin sets them apart and above the other skin colors there are in this world. Our white ancestors arrived in America four hundred years ago and felt entitled to push the Indians west and grab every piece of their land that they left behind. Having taken all the land from the Indians east of the Mississippi River, the white folk proceeded west using the Army to kill off the remaining Indians in the far west. The buffalo hunters slaughtered millions of buffalo in order to starve the Indians. The U.S. government signed over five hundred treaties over a two hundred year period that forced most of the remaining Indian tribes onto reservations many of which were unfit for human habitation, and still, we have yet to honor any of these treaties. No, if skin color is going to determine who would make the best rulers of this land it surely wouldn't be the white race.

I do not know or understand how some people think skin color should make any significant difference between any of us humans other than to denote the beautiful skin color differences we have with one another. Having said that, I am however, very conscious of my white skin every time I am following a car driven by a person of color. In seconds I note how they are being extra careful not to go over a solid line or one MPH over the speed limit and everyone knows why this is the case here in our country.

For the most part, there will not be any white, black, brown, or yellow skinned people on Earth in a thousand years … we will have comingled ourselves into a color we have yet to know and we will truly have become the Earth people God created us to be.

I lived in Brazil for several years and was amused to see on some applications how they listed the usual races; Negro, Indio, Blanco, Latino, and Otro (other). Most Brazilians chose 'Otro' for they felt they were no longer any of the colors listed because they'd been comingling their races for the last four hundred years which has resulted in them having beautiful skin textures and colors; someday it'll be that way for all of us and it cannot happen soon enough!

We as a nation need to look at the different methods used by law enforcement when policing people of color because there is a difference and we all know it.

Most people of color are always on their toes making sure they don't violate any motor vehicle rules, local ordinances, or state laws that white people never give a thought to; we all know why because this is passive racism.

It was never like this when I was growing up in New England in the fifties, but of course, the fifties were very different to the lay of the land today. No matter, the tactics some police officers use to apprehend people of color vs a white person are not the same across our land and therein lies the rub.

Some police departments authorize apprehension tactics like choke holds, baton beatings, non-stop tasing, or the use of lethal force when the person they are trying to apprehend may not even have a weapon. The police officers in the fifties used the Argus Claw to apprehend a suspect or an extremely agitated person, but the claw was declared cruel and abusive. So, now we let the police use deadly force because police officers don't want to get too close to the suspect if they don't have to, and yet, even when they are close why do some police officers choose to make a kill shot vs a shot to the shoulder, legs, or arms to neutralize the suspect. Could it be that some officers lack the courage to get too close or is it that some of them have a killer instinct? An MMPI test would bring this front and center.

It's also plain to see on many of the videos taken that there is more in play when some police officers are approaching a person of color who may have been stopped for a motor vehicle infraction. It quickly develops from a routine traffic stop to where the cop is drawing his gun and the person of color is so frightened that they have bolted from their car running for their life followed by the cop firing shots at them in their back. Blacks can see all of this coming while they are getting pulled over! Maybe there should be a number for people of color to call in the FBI as soon as they are being pulled over so the dialogue between the person of color and police officer can be monitored for what should or should not be taking place.

A 60 Minutes segment explained what happens when police in some jurisdictions arrive at a scene where there is an overly agitated person. They are allowed to make a judgment call declaring the person is in a state of 'excitable delirium' and request an EMT or medic to administer a Ketamine injection, a powerful anesthetic that could have deadly consequences. The entire medical world has voiced deep skepticism as to whether there is such a condition. It seems the police in Minneapolis have a 3000 percent increase in the use of Ketamine with these type of encounters over the last 7 years. So, what is it that the police are trying to avoid when it comes to handling these types of issues or could it just be that when President Reagan did away with funding our national mental health care facilities in 1981 there is no place for the police to take these excited individuals except to jail. More so, what do some police officers not have in the way of training that should be part and parcel of every police force? Some communities take a more personal interest in the training of their police force. I met a man in Eau Claire, Wisconsin who was becoming a police officer. He shared that he had to attend fifteen AA and Alanon meetings before he could graduate from the Eau Claire Police Academy. This is what is meant by going an extra mile that will make all the difference in a town's police officers.

Joe Biden, our newly elected president is right when he says there are bad apples in some of our police departments. There are also some police departments that are so pressured by the police unions to where they cannot terminate a police officer for using unnecessary or deadly force or even suspend a police officer for continued violations of the police guidelines set forth by the state. There are many localities across the land that do not use a citizen review board as an oversight review measure whenever a citizen has been killed by a police officer to at least determine if the case should go before a grand jury.

Maybe the time has come to re-train police departments in the art of using less lethal policing procedures and re-adopt tools such as the Argus claw. My best friend was a police officer in the Boston area in the 60's and he told me there were numerous times the claw saved the day and a life when he and his partner were apprehending a fugitive or an overly excited person who was out of control; especially in domestic violence or barroom situations. On one occasion when he and his partner were called to break up a fight in a barroom he was knocked to the floor but managed to get the claw on the ankle of the customer that knocked him down. He brought that person down onto his knees squealing for mercy while his partner cuffed him. I let him test the claw on my arm and the pain was excruciating in a split second. My friend was an ex-combat veteran and didn't shrink from using physical force, but when that failed he would bring the suspect down with the claw every time; he managed his fear and he never shot and killed a person in 35 years on the force. This was a major metropolitan crime area and his partner for twenty years was a black policeman.

We've all seen the armed white supremists and American Nazi members in the Charlottesville streets on TV during their 'Unite the Right' protest movement in 2017. Images showed counter protesters trying to prevent these armed crowds from continuing their march through their community that ended with a young woman being run down by one of the radical protesters in a car. President Trump announced on TV that both sides were at fault and would not strike a blow at the white supremists or Nazi movement. How could he, he was indebted to them! This in and of itself was a showcase moment of what we could expect from Trump as president.

Trump's grandfather marched in a KKK parade in New York City in 1914 which gives us all an inside view to some of the conversations this family must have had over dinner during the last 100 years. The Trump real estate businesses were constantly being sued in court by the NAACP for violating the civil rights of NYC blacks who had been told such and such property was no longer for rent when it actually may have been still for rent.

So, it is plain for us to see that Trump is a chip off the family block with respect to racism, but he may not be an avid racist. He does however know how to play the racist card in politics by showing off blacks at his rallies and surrounding himself with high profile black professionals and business leaders. He also knows how to butter up the white supremists at his rallies to keep them in tow.

Trump is addicted to power, and doesn't give a hoot one way or another about white supremists and their hatred for people of color, the Jews, and the Muslims. He caters to the white supremist image and wants his supporters to think he has their backs only when the racism card is played. Trump uses the racist card when he has the country on the ropes and seems to be inches away of establishing himself as the autocratic leader of the USA. Almost any American in 2016 would've said, "No" to this premise, but not so today. So, I submit that all of this white supremist and anarchist posturing is dangerous business and will continue to come into play when it benefits Trump or leaders like him.

There's another area in our society that we need to look at that I believe is severely impacting us as a nation; discipline or the lack thereof for our children.

I was somewhat of a class clown when I was in high school and to some degree it affected my grades. I got my driver's license just before my junior year and my stepfather agreed to let me buy a car. He stipulated that I had to agree that if I didn't improve my deportment or conduct in school the plates for the car were coming off. I agreed not believing this would ever happen.

Well, wouldn't you know how full of myself I became with having my own car in the fifties and before I knew it report cards came out. I got a D in conduct! I came home from school, put my report card on the kitchen table, and got ready to go to my afternoon job.

When I went to get into my car I noticed the rear plate was missing. I went back into the house and told my stepfather. He said, "I took it off and I just don't understand why you're not wanting to drive your car." I yelled, "I do want to drive my car!" ... "Doesn't look thataway! You agreed to give up the plate if you got a bad mark in conduct and you did get a failing mark in conduct."

I was livid when I had to board the city bus to go to work and school for the next 90 days. If I sat around with a long face at home I was told to leave the room. I had to endure the discipline meted out for the next three months. The conduct mark on my report card three months later was B+, the grades on all my studies improved, and my stepfather put the plates back on my car. This was a great life lesson for me that carried me through the rest of my adult life.

This has not been the case for most kids for the last 60 years. Most parents are unable to follow through with discipline for more than a day or two and the children suffer the consequences of this because they're not becoming adults. Kids that haven't been wisely disciplined do not reach full maturity and the worst part is that they too will not be able to discipline their kids when they're married. Remember, there's a difference between discipline and mean spirited punishment! A great deal of what's going on in America right now can be attributed to undisciplined kids growing up to be undisciplined adults. This along with the fact that none of our children are being drafted to serve in the military means they're never going to comingle with strangers from all over our country and receive or understand the merits of camaraderie and discipline with their fellow Americans. I'll say no more on this issue other than the draft was a good path for us to learn how to comingle with fellow Americans from all walks of life, become disciplined adults, and respect one another which is something we are terribly lacking today.

Chapter 17

It would be ludicrous or close to being insane for any human being living anywhere on this planet to suggest that there's nothing wrong with our weather, the oceans, our drinking water, our breathing air, or our atmosphere. The poorest of the poor have no survival options against the wind driven droughts, lack of water, rising sea levels are overflowing into the rice paddies, walkways in Venice are a foot under water, and tornados are ripping across the plains in the U.S. at a rate never before seen. Most folks don't care who is to blame, they just want the world leaders to err on the side of safety and start doing something.

Most cities along the coastlines pumped their sanitary waste to sea for over a 100 years before the advent of waste treatment facilities. I am not that naïve to think that some of those city leaders thought this was a sensible idea or that this wasn't going to harm the ocean water or the creatures that lived there. They did so because it was an inexpensive fix.

In the mid-1990's I was overseeing the construction of a power plant in Colombia and I would travel to and from the project every other week by air from Miami. When the aircraft began its decent I would look out the window of the plane and see what had to be one of the worse ongoing environmental disasters in the world. A battleship gray colored plume began where a river met the coast and went 100 miles out into the azure blue Caribbean; it took my breath away every time I saw it. How was it possible for this to continue? Surely tens of thousands of airline passengers saw this same site from the windows of every plane that was going to land or had just taken off from this same airport every year.

Multiply these two locations by several thousand around the world and you have an environmental nightmare that is beyond comprehension, especially when you can imagine the environmental destruction that is taking place below the surface of these affected bodies of water throughout the world. Every day fishermen in these affected areas set out to sea in their commercial and privately owned fishing boats to harvest fish from these environmentally compromised bodies of water around the world as if there were absolutely no risks to the consumer.

And lets not forget the plastic island the size of Texas that's floating around on top of the Pacific Ocean someplace. This island of plastic trash mostly from Asia acts as a reflector further raising the temperature underneath the ozone layer. No country has stepped up to do anything about correcting this as if it really matters at this point who was responsible for causing this catastrophe because we are all affected by it no matter who caused it!

Then there's the terrible weather that has been increasing across the U.S. for the last ten years. Fires raging in California, one storm cell after another leaving a state of continuous flooding and property destruction not to mention the hundreds of tornados that wreak havoc on a scale never before experienced across the plains. This year we've gone through the entire alphabet twice for the first time in history in order to name all the hurricanes.

The world's leading scientists and climatologists predict the oceans will rise another 3 to 7 feet in the next 30 years, not

100 years as previously thought and you would never know from the way people are still building along the coastlines; makes one wonder what they know that the rest of don't.

Most people don't read the scientific reviews about what's happening in Antarctica. The scientists there have discovered that the Pacific Ocean waters have been flowing in and under and around a glacier that sits on the massive Antarctica land mass to where they are very concerned that a section of the glacier the size of Florida may slip off the land causing all the oceans and seas throughout the world to rise 5 to 15 feet. This would be a catastrophe causing huge numbers of the world's population to make a mad dash to higher ground, and for sure they would not be welcomed by some of the folks that live on the higher ground!

I met a doctor on a flight who was going to a conference in Boston for Children's Pulmonary diseases some years back. He asked what I did for a living and when I told him that I was managing the construction of large coal fired power plants around the world he took out an overlay from his briefcase that he said he was going to show on the big screen at the conference. The sketch showed a large light bulb shaped area imposed on a map of the United States that began in Kansas and proceeded up into the northeast enveloping the New England states and down along the coast to the Middle Atlantic states and the light bulb shape was all shaded in gray. He said there were three million kids with asthma living inside this area that had severe breathing issues caused by the increase of small particulates from the flue gas emissions from all the stacks of all the coal burning power plants in this area. These particulates traveled through the air and ended up being inhaled into the small airways in children's lungs. Talk about being embarrassed. Most professionals in the power generation industry knew that bag house filters would have prevented the smaller particles, SO2, and CO2 from escaping, but companies weren't willing to make the investment. To make matters worse, in 2004, GW Bush issued an executive order that relieved all coal fired plants from having to comply with the Clean Air Act deadline of 2006 which allowed some of these coal fired plants to continue belching these harmful flue gases right up to today. This was all about wanting to make even more of a profit while they put the public's health and these children with asthma in harm's way.

In 1954, the utility companies in the fourteen most eastern states produced 41,000 megawatts of power each and every day. In 1960, just six years later, these same states produced 320,000 megawatts of power every day. This tenfold increase was happening throughout the world, but nowhere as fast as it was in the more advanced countries like the United States. Scientists have zeroed in on this being when the earth's temperature began to rise and adverse climate conditions began to occur. We became power gluttons and there is no doubt that we were all complicit! We just weren't paying attention!

Scientists discovered that coal mining itself releases huge amounts of methane gas that affects our climate even worse than CO2. This methane gas is 80 times more harmful to our atmosphere than carbon dioxide.

It took 450 million years for the final geological and atmospheric adaptive processes to be completed in order for Earth to be ready for us and all the other living species that were going to dwell here and we have compromised the entire environmental landscape in just the past 175 years. The worse part is that many of us have yet to believe any of this is true or our fault and to make matters worse have demonized anyone that suggests that we are complicit. Many of us have aligned themselves with political forces that have created policies and supported leaders who want to avoid any financial recriminations or liabilities to correct our environmental shortcomings, and yet, we all know deep down that we must do something if we and our future off-spring expect to continue living here on this planet and wouldn't it be best for us to err on the side of safety? Our future offspring are not going to be able to breathe dirty air, drink impure water, and be healthy too!

President Trump wasted no time pulling the United States out of the Paris Climate Accords in 2017. Why! Because Trump says he doesn't want to hurt American workers; rubbish! The GOP claims these are normal earth transients and they have not been caused by us humans and it doesn't make any sense for us to expend funds to eradicate something that we humans are not responsible for doing that are just normal transient changes occurring with the planet itself. More rubbish!

How peculiar it was for President Trump to set November 3, 2020, Election Day, as the date to finalize our exit from the Paris Climate Accords. This act makes the U.S. the only nation in the world to do so. If you ponder all of this and determine that the GOP is correct in their assessment, this would mean that the 185 countries that signed the Paris Accords are not correct which would then suggest that America has some seriously dysfunctional rationale and immoral persuasions. Many corporations in the U.S are only backing politicians who will not support climate change policies that will adversely affect their profit margins. In addition, there are those Americans that have more of an investment in a political party and their ideologies than they do to each other's well-being which is a much deeper problem than climate change and way beyond anything that I will be discussing in this book!

While you are reading this book, there are 14 super tankers traveling the seas to countries around the world loading, transporting, and unloading crude oil and refined oil products. These 14 ships emit more pollution from their huge bunker sea oil burning boilers a year than the emissions from all the automobiles on Earth in one year. There is boiler technology available that could eliminate 50 percent of these harmful emissions if the leaders of our world would only come together and mandate these changes.

A polar vortex descended through the central states into Texas this past weekend leaving millions without electricity or water in frigid cold temperatures for four days. Governor Abbott immediately proclaimed the renewable and green energy sectors supported by the liberals were to blame for the collapse of the entire Texas power system known as the Ercot. The Texas utility companies quickly contradicted this statement and informed the public that many of the power plants failed because they were not sufficiently winterized to withstand the frigid cold snap.

Renewable and green energy are only used to supplement or temporarily replace the power generated by fossil or nuclear power plants. Solar power facilities cannot generate power during overcast weather or at night time. Wind turbines cannot produce power without wind and may even have to shut down when the winds are too high. This means that we must have ample steam driven turbines connected to generators that will provide all the power we need 24/7 across our entire grid. Further investigation might reveal that many if not all of the fossil fuel power plants in Texas that were not able to stay online was due to a lack of proper winterization of the plants. Additional investigation might reveal there is little to no amount of standby capacity in the system during normal peak conditions. Natural gas suppliers also failed to winterize some of their facilities. The utility companies failed to make the necessary investments to winterize the power plants that would have enabled them to remain in service as is possible in the northern latitudes. This also could be the case with many power generating facilities throughout the south that have not deemed it necessary to winterize their systems as well. The Texas event gives us a heads up of what we can expect if these future polar vortexes become common as this is how the Earth is going to cool itself down when temperatures get too high.

So, when you flick a light switch or turn on the AC, you are part of the problem and you are taking part in advancing destructive climate change via the leaders you send to Washington DC that may not believe climate change is caused by us. If each of us can get honest enough to where we can admit that we in some small part do in fact cause climate damage, then we can use the ballot box to elect leaders who also agree. If we want Earth to be available for future generations to live on, then we must vote for those leaders who are not kept in power by powerful corporations that do not want to err on the side of safety, and do not want to make the necessary investments to return the environment of our planet to the way it was before we embarked on the industrial revolution that eventually began to destroy our eco systems.

Yes, we are making great technological advances in the power generation and automobile industries, but until we mine coal safely, put bag houses on all coal burning power plants, construct more nuclear plants, and enact laws to promote positive environmentally favorable changes that will reward our eco structure, we will continue to harm our planet.

Chapter 18

After removing all of Obama's policies during Trump's first month in office ... four years of few policy changes ... several failed attempts at removing the Affordable Care Act without a replacement if it was removed ... no attempt to enact any gun control measures on who should or should not be able to purchase guns ... our NATO partners and our allies are still on the ropes with respect to President Trump's relations with Putin, Saudi Arabia, Israel, Turkey, China, N. Korea, and Iran ... a failed tariff war ... some of our trading partners looking elsewhere ... tax revenue shortfalls for the last 14 months ... two back to back stimulus bills totaling almost $4 trillion dollars that have been added to the debt ... a broken justice department ... a pandemic that continues to take American lives and devastate our economy; we have finally changed leaders.

This may be a good time with respect to the debt to see how the Fed plans on paying all our bills due to the Covid virus and what may lie ahead on the horizon for us in the dollar world.

The Central bank and Treasury are printing (electronically-not paper) trillions of dollars and it's come time for us to turn our attention to the nation's financial situation and the Federal Reserve reaction to all of what has been going on. We need always maintain our oversight on the Fed, the Treasury, and the banks to make sure what they are doing will not affect us adversely.

We've got some hard decisions to make because we are looking at some severe economic changes that are about to take place that were not attended to by Trump and that have unknown durations due to the Covid-19 virus, revenue shortfalls, stimulus relief, tariff war, and servicing of our debt that need immediate attention.

The Biden administration will need to review the outgoing administration's plan to print money, pay every bill, guarantee every debt, insure that no fixed income investor loses money, and to ensure all of the above will not lead to darker skies ahead.

The Trump Labor Department has not been all that truthful as to how many Americans are currently unemployed, but it's looking like there are approximately 20 million people that were forced out of work due to the virus. This is more than all of the 2008 Great Recession which means millions of autos could be repossessed, people could be evicted from apartments, hundreds of thousands of mortgages could fail, thousands of small businesses could close their doors, millions of unpaid utility bills, billions in credit card debt could go unpaid. This doesn't include a long list of major corporations that have been severely impacted by the Covid virus.

The Fed's plan is to reimburse everyone connected to each of these setbacks which means companies and holders of these loans will be reimbursed as well, and airlines and hotels for example will not have to file for bankruptcy. That's a lot of money!

The Fed also plans on propping up the municipal, corporate, and Treasury bond markets. The Treasury authorized $2 trillion in the first stimulus bill and in order to do that the Fed is buying up all the debt that the Treasury will be selling. The Fed will then print (electronically) new money and give it to the holder of the Treasury debt. Banks can convert some of these reserves to cash and payments as they see fit.

The Fed creates reserves in normal times by buying T-bills which then gives them an asset against a liability; the money will keep inflation to a minimum. All of the above is lending power, not spending power.

This can get a bit dicey! What will happen if the loans aren't repaid? The Treasury will take the first 5 to 10 percent of the losses and because the Treasury gets its money from the Fed, it really will come back as printed money. If Fed's losses are severe then the Treasury will have to recapitalize the Fed with free T-bills.

An example ... if a bakery borrows money to buy a larger oven, the bakery will make more bread and use the extra profit to pay back the loan on the oven and if it doesn't the bank owns the oven.

It's been 30 days since Biden won the election and President Trump has yet to concede the election, in fact. he's taken to using his team of lawyers and what he thinks are his courts especially if they have sitting judges that he appointed to get even more of the election results over turned.

Biden had a 7 million plurality vote margin of victory, however, he only won Wisconsin, Pennsylvania, Georgia, Arizona, and Nevada electorate votes by a very narrow margin; 158,000 votes with 155 million people having voted. Trump won the 2016 electoral vote by an even slimmer margin when you consider 130 million people voted. It shows the country was divided before that election and now even more so.

The third wave of the Covid virus is raging with 2500 people dying every day and 160,000 new cases every day and that doesn't include the anticipated spike from the two million people that ignored the CDC plea not to travel over the Thanksgiving holiday that is about to come into play.

The Dow Jones average went over the 30,000 point mark for the first time which may indicate that some of the companies and businesses hit hard by this pandemic are not on the NYSE.

A week before Christmas we received word that was confirmed by Secretary of State Pompei that the Russians have had unfettered access into all of our strategic computer systems ranging from our nuclear weapon systems, armed forces, and Homeland Security; Trump disputes it was the Russians and says it was the Chinese.

Maybe it's time Trump's base received an education on what Mr. Putin has been up to in the way of espionage for the last twenty years. In 2002, Putin sent six Russian teams to the U.S. that melted into our fabric as everyday husbands and wives in order to acquire strategic information on our nuclear weapon systems. The FBI kept tabs on them from the time they got off the plane and over the next eight years. They rounded them all up in 2010 and made a swap for one of our agents that was being held in Russia, but Russia did not get any information on our weapons systems. Russia however did manage during this eight month long cyber-attack to extract some of our most strategic secrets on all our military and government data systems that might allow Putin to be able to make some calculated assessments on our defense systems as to whether or not we are vulnerable to a first strike. This is the most dangerous it has ever been between us and Russia for 75 years. We may never know the connection between Trump and Putin and it may be too late to rectify the damages caused by Mr. Trump having turned a blind eye to Putin, but what's really sad about the entire mess is that his supporters either don't understand this or they don't believe a word of it; but they do believe Trump when he says it was China not Russia. How would he know that when he doesn't read any of his classified daily briefs? This is beyond sad and further confirmation that stupid is what stupid does!

President Elect Joe Biden and his team of advisors are keeping an eye on the two U.S. Senator runoffs in Georgia that will take place on January 5, 2021 which will determine if the U.S. Senate will remain under the GOP control. If it does, you can be sure it's going to be a repeat performance of what took place after the 2010 midterm that gave the GOP the Senate for the next six years of the Obama administration. It will also be an uphill battle for Biden to get anything done that's going to need Senate approval unless there are a few GOP Senators willing to vote support cross the aisle or continued use and abuse of Executive Power to get things done.

The first use of Executive Power was when Congress was out of session and George Washington used his executive power on April 22, 1793 to instruct federal officers to arrest and prosecute citizens who interfered with the war between France and England. Sadly, this practice has been abused to where presidents opt more often than not to use Executive Power when they know Congress or the Senate will not vote in their favor otherwise nothing would get done, and worse, this is not what the founders envisioned.

U.S. trade and tariff policies have hampered our trade relations with Asia. The U.S. will not be a member of the new 11 member Comprehensive and Aggressive Trans-Pacific Partnership that now includes China who was not included in the TPP trade agreement in 2016. The Biden team should make every effort to determine if it would be wise for the U.S. to seek membership and that of course is if we would even be welcomed into this Partnership.

The Covid virus began in China and yet they did not reach 100,000 cases or 5000 deaths. This allowed China's manufacturing base and world trade to continue almost as it normally would and proved to the world why wearing masks and distancing pays off. Chinese exchange students and espionage agents continue to spy and steal our military secrets, manufacturing technologies, scientific break throughs, and new discoveries via direct espionage. The Biden team needs to review and clamp down on which Chinese student exchange and cultural programs are not in our best interest; this is and should be a top priority for the incoming Biden team to put a stop to the U.S. hemorrhaging of our scientific and manufacturing break throughs to China.

The Constitution of the United States is a text that was written 234 years ago to help guide our newly proclaimed Republic after patriots just like you and I won the Revolutionary War. The text in the Constitution has never changed. It is not by any means a perfect document nor has there been any American that has perfectly understood it; it was written to help us manage this newfound way of governing called democracy where we were all going to have a part in electing those that would lead us and manage our governmental affairs and obligations.

We have managed to stay together for the last 234 years despite one of the worst civil wars that ever took place on this planet, WW I, the Spanish Flu, the Great Depression, WW II, the Cold War with Russia, the Great Recession, and the Covid-19 virus which proves we've had the moxie so far, but do we as a nation have the willingness to continue hammering out this gift on the anvil of time in order to form an even more perfect union to save it.

Ruth Bader Ginsburg, Supreme Court Justice for the last 27 years died on September 18, 2020. She knew the Republicans would not postpone or defer her replacement as was done when Justice Scalia died in 2016. Senator McConnell is still smarting from when the Democrats chose not to approve Judge Bork for the Supreme Court in 1987. The Democrats voted against Bork for fear he was going to roll back civil rights. In 1991, HW Bush nominated Judge Thomas for the Supreme Court and towards the end of the vetting process, Anita Hill, a former intern for Thomas testified that he had shown her pornographic pictures and she was frightened that he did so to have sex with her; Thomas was approved although most Americans felt her story was truthful and compelling. In 2018 when President Trump nominated Brett Kavanaugh to the Supreme Court bench, Christine Blasey Ford, a student who attended college with Kavanaugh testified that in 1982 he attempted to rape her at a party. She was followed by several other women who also accused Kavanaugh of similar sexual assaults around the same period. Most Americans felt Christine's testimony was truthful and over the hill compelling, and yet Senator McConnell held a session in the Senate wherein he convinced the GOP senators otherwise and even threatened a few senators that he would run a candidate against them in a primary. Now this kind of behavior should warrant expulsion from the Senate period!

Senator McConnell spent his entire career as a U.S. Senator planning and exacting revenge for what happened to Bork, Thomas, and now Kavanaugh; a sad epitaph of revenge at its worse, especially when there was credible testimony against two of the court nominees. For reasons I cannot fathom and will never know why, revenge runs deep with the GOP party which reinforces the need for all our elected officials to undergo an MMPI examination that would surely reveal issues such as this.

RBG was right. As soon as Senator McConnell heard she died he called Trump and advised him to nominate Amy Barrett and Trump wasted no time announcing her candidacy for SCOTUS. Few Americans knew that Senator McConnell nominated Amy Barrett to the Court of Appeals 7th Circuit three years before knowing then that she had no experience as a sitting judge in a lower court. McConnell has so politicized the Supreme Court nomination and approval process that it has undermined the functionality of the court!

The Democrats were livid because after Chief Justice Scalia died in 2016 which was a presidential election year, the Republican controlled Senate would not conduct any hearings to fill the seat by a candidate appointed by President Obama; democrats proclaimed this wasn't fair.

The truth is, it has been this way for 22 of the 29 Justices appointed to the Supreme Court since 1869 which means a nominee would have to be nominated and approved either before the election or in the lame-duck period before the next presidential inauguration. That total is now 30 after Amy

Lee Barrett was sworn in to replace Justice Ruth Bader Ginsburg.

Of those 29 times, a vacancy on the high court occurred in an election year 19 times and presidents nominated a successor when their party controlled the Senate. In those cases, the Senate majority party confirmed their president's nomination 17 times.

So, there you have it. The appointing, approving, and filling a Supreme Court vacancy is one of the most contentious and politicized undertakings in our government and because this is the system we have inherited, both political parties have successfully twisted the intent of the text in the Constitution to determine a judicial outcome via SCOTUS which is politics at its worse. We need to enact an amendment to prevent further misuse of this precious body.

Chief Justice Roberts announced on 12/8/20 that the Supreme Court would not be weighing in on the GOP view that the election process in several swing states was rigged.

We are so fortunate today to be able to search Yahoo, Google, or Wikipedia for the truth before we get all riled up and embroiled in heated political discussions which sometimes really isn't about politics; it's just the way it is and has been since we became a Republic. The media could have done better making sure everyone knew the SCOTUS history of replacing justices as well.

Rather than both parties having a similar vision for America going forward we have two parties with absolutely no common policies because they each have a different view of what they'd like America to look like and who was going to pay for it. Patsies don't ever find it necessary to get involved with the details until it's too late.

So, you need to ask yourself, 'Which party do I want to tie my wagon to? Should we have a four party system? In the meantime, what is the Republican, Independent, or Democratic party going to do for me that will be in mine and our nation's best interest? Why do I continue voting for a party that doesn't care a fig about me and my future? These are the questions a patsy will normally never ask himself or herself because when you do it implies there are some changes needed to be made. It implies that you are going to have to become active, get honest, and get involved if you and your family are going to have a happy and fulfilling life here in America and what would be so bad about that?

With respect to the last four years with Trump as our president, I hope historians will be able to write that this was a turning point and one of the most beneficial periods in our history because it helped some of us realize how precious a gift this democracy is and how close we came to losing it!

If you still haven't gotten off the train, I am going to ask you to go and sit in a quiet place. I want you to contemplate what it is you would want our leaders to do that would most improve the quality of life for all of us as a whole. Write down what you find and see which political party and candidates talk about these issues.

Chapter 19

There were 118.9 million workers employed in the U.S. before the beginning of President Bill Clinton's 1st term in 1992 and 137.6 million people employed by the end of his 2nd term in 2000, almost 20 million new jobs! This was a government that was really doing something for the well-being and welfare of its citizens! And yet, only one side of the political leadership had accomplished this; the GOP had dug their heels in and were having nothing to do with working or compromising with the Democrats. Ring a bell? This all or nothing approach by the GOP has been going on for 60 years.

This was also the last time our country adhered to practicing prudent taxation and spending measures. Bill Clinton was president and he introduced the Omnibus Reconciliation Act in 1993 which was opposed by almost every GOP member in the House and Senate. The top federal income tax rate increased from 31% to 39.6%. The bill included $255 billion in spending cuts over a five-year period. The effects of the bill helped the US federal government to experience its first budget surplus since the 1960s. President Clinton presided over eight years of steady growth without adding to the debt and created a 63 billion dollar surplus. The number of welfare recipients fell by 59% from 12.2 million to 4.9 million people during this same period.

GW Bush followed Clinton but not his spending or revenue policies and over the next 8 years the debt rose 8 trillion dollars. He also turned a blind eye to 70,000 corporations that relocated their factories overseas in order to improve their profit margins which led to the loss of 3.8 million jobs.

GW Bush was diametrically opposed to Clinton's policies which left the middle class marginalized. He increased the wealth of the already wealthy and well to do Americans with two tax cuts during his two terms. Some of these well to do folks are those cross over voters from the other two parties that I talked about that the GOP needs to maintain control of their power. They overlooked his invasion of Iraq as if this had nothing to do with them when in fact it had everything to do with them. I gave the voters that re-elected GW Bush in 2004 an F- after he had already signed two tax cuts and launched us into a $4 trillion war in Iraq.

I keep reminding everyone that the wealthy people paid a 72% tax on their earnings from 1945 to 1980 which paid down the debt from WW II, Korean War, Vietnam War, and the Cold war which totaled $15.8 trillion dollars. In 1980 the debt was down to $985 billion and the tax was lowered by Reagan on the wealthy to 50% which was good. He should have left it there for another two years and we would have celebrated being debt free and thanked the wealthy for their part. No, he had to cut the taxes on the wealthy again to 38% and that was the end of us ever being that close to being debt free. Reagan had to borrow $3 trillion before he left office to maintain the budget. Ninety percent of us Americans had been played!

We are in this financial pickle because the GOP believes the wealthy should be able to keep all the money they earn and the budget be damned! We the voters must decide if we want to tie our wagon to a party that has recklessly pursued this policy because if the wealthy are not paying higher taxes that they can well afford, we must cut back on the spending and become a 2nd or 3rd rate country that we are beginning to act and look like anyways. If you think we've had some hard knocks over the last 20 years you haven't seen anything if we don't get our debt paid down. In the meantime, don't believe them when they tell you debt is good; it isn't! You'll notice I wrote 'our debt' even though the tax relief money went to the wealthy because they are not paying their fair share!

It does little good for us voters when we take to switching our support from one party to other every four to eight years. We end up with new political leadership that have the same old policies that remove or repeal all the changes and executive orders made by the proceeding party. The incoming party sets about re-enacting new bills, executive orders, and legislation that meets their same old philosophies and policies that are opposite to the outgoing party. We go on and repeat this cycle every four to eight years with little to no thought process in between; this is not what the founders had in mind when they began this Republic. It's nothing more than a good cop bad cop system that does not serve the people. No wonder autocratic forms of government have become appealing to some Americans. Most of the gridlock starts with tax relief and the craziest part is there is barely or never enough money to meet the budgets. The last tax cut in 2017 reduced our budget revenue by almost a $2.3 trillion dollars.

We will not survive if we don't have the revenues to pay our bills and pay down our debt. We owe 27 trillion dollars because the GOP since 1981 has granted six such tax cuts to the wealthy and has had to borrow this money to replace those tax losses which means we will have paid $7.5 trillion servicing the interest on the debt alone which is about what the rich have been given in tax cuts over the last 30 years. The wealthy should be paying a 50% tax rate until such time as the debt is paid off. We the people need to nominate, elect and send leaders to manage our federal government that will force each administration to create and maintain balanced budgets and maintain a minimal debt. We cannot have our cake and eat it too. Cities, counties, and states do not manage their fiscal responsibilities with such recklessness and neither should the federal government. It's one thing to disagree on policies and it's another to keep on behaving like jackasses and it's We the voters that allow this to continue!

The Covid virus became a major embarrassment when our healthcare facilities ran out of critical healthcare equipment and we found out that most of it was being manufactured overseas. This resulted in every healthcare facility in the U.S. having to reuse expendable masks and gloves for the first six months of the pandemic. Once again, we shot ourselves in the foot by electing leaders who let corporations overseen by inconsiderate and bottom line CEO's that put us all in harm's way. There is nothing wrong with corporations making a good profit using overseas inexpensive labor as long as there are emergency measures and supplies in place that will tide us over until we can manufacture these must have commodities here in the U.S. Short sighted behavior fueled by greed will never work!

When President Reagan informed us that having a national debt was good for our country, we we're being played. Remember, the GOP party does not have enough party members to elect anyone; voters from the Independent and Democratic parties have to cross over. Most were surprised when it became clear that Reagan's policies were not serving the majority of the country and yet they still re-elected him in 1984 which left the middleclass with a paltry 2.8 percent wage increase over eight years which became Reagan's famous trickledown economics. This is exactly what takes place when we become patsies or don't show up to vote.

This has never been about politics ... it's always been about the misuse of our money by some politicians who want us to turn a blind eye to their misuse of power in order to keep their seats around the table of power. They continue to keep us all worked up against one another so they can go about the business of making our country into their business. Wake up! Stop voting candidates into power that are always promising you what they're never going to deliver and we end up being played to where we start fighting amongst ourselves which keeps our eyes of the bouncing ball.

President Biden has been in power for one month. His vaccination program is on schedule and his plan to have 300 million of us vaccinated by July is on schedule. He wants to sign a $1.9 trillion stimulus package that is supported by most economists and members of both parties. The GOP began digging their heals in and Republican Senator Johnson from Wisconsin is going to read the entire bill which will take up to 12 hours for no reason other than he can. Childish and disgusting! Remember this when it's time to vote in the 2022 election!

The wealthy paid a 72% tax rate from 1945 until 1981 and they were still 1,000 percent more well off than most Americans. We would not have been able to pay down the debt from WW II and the Cold War otherwise.

The wealthy are going to have to pay higher taxes again or we are going to become a 2nd rate country; we can't have it both ways! End of story!

The middleclass voters cannot continue electing GOP leaders that go to Washington DC to serve those that are well off already. We have to elect leaders that are going to think out of the box and actually represent all of us. We must elect leaders who will perform their duties in accordance to the oath they swear to protect our constitution ... duty, honor, and country!

Chapter 20

It's been 39 days since the election. President Trump has not conceded and continues to proclaim the election was rigged and a fraud. Seventeen GOP States Attorney Generals enjoined with Texas AG Ted Paxton to petition the Supreme Court to overturn the election results in Michigan, Wisconsin, Pennsylvania, and Georgia by negating 10 million votes from those four states. The Supreme Court wasted no time handing down a scathing 9-0 rebuke and letting the results of the election stand which is another way of saying our election results are not negotiable! I wish this had been the case in the 2000 election.

Various GOP factions including the president made over 60 attempts to overturn the election results which the lower courts labeled frivolous. National polls show 70 percent of the GOP voters back these baseless claims which means they too are poor losers.

One hundred and thirty members of the GOP Congressional caucus filed a brief in support of the Texas petition to the Supreme Court to overturn the 2020 election results which means they too have become spoilers who have more of an investment in winning than they do for our democracy; they would never have been elected if their constituents had used due diligence to determine if they had the moral fiber to defend the Constitution.

At this juncture, not one GOP election supervisor in any of the fifty states noted any significant improprieties at any of their polls during the voting or counting processes throughout the entire election process. Talk about selfishness and immaturity of the GOP voters for not having gotten their way; it further proves why our founders did not want to give everyone the right to vote. The DEM voters might have been off the wall upset at Trump winning the 2016 election but they didn't start complaining that the election was rigged or petition the courts to get it nullified; they acted like grown-ups.

The third spike of the Covid virus includes many of the two million people who traveled over the Thanksgiving holiday against the advice of the CDC. The virus is raging across America with no letup in sight. Much of this is due to the Covid propaganda aired by Trump and lack of scientific oversight. Hospital ICU's and ER's across the land are at or over 100 percent capacity with some hospitals releasing non-virus patients early to make space for the virus cases. President Trump proclaims the credit for getting the pharmaceuticals into warp speed to engineer and manufacture vaccines but takes no responsibility for the pandemic overrunning our country.

America let out a loud 'phew' followed by a "thank you!" to the Supreme Court for doing the next right thing, but that hasn't stopped several rogue GOP Senators and 130 Congressional leaders from rejecting Biden as the winner of the 2020 election! They now plan to reject the certification of the electoral vote on January 6th that has already been signed off by all fifty states which translates into them having more of a political investment in Trump than they do to the oath they swore to uphold the Constitution. The idea that they were willing to compromise the vote count ceremonies that have been going on for the last 244 years in order to remain in Trump's graces is a disgrace and they should lose their congressional seats. Now I understand why the founders thought it was a good idea to have term limits!

There were seven GOP leaders that did honor their oaths they took to protect our constitution from our enemies that in this case happened to be domestic. Republicans Senators Richard Burr from North Carolina, Bill Cassidy from Louisiana, Susan Collins from Maine, Lisa Murkowski from Alaska, Mitt Romney from Utah, Ben Sasse from Nebraska, and Pat Toomey from Pennsylvania stood tall and voted with the Democrats to impeach President Donald Trump. Scathing editorials and Fox News criticized them for undermining the GOP and throwing away their political careers. But these were exactly the type of leaders that prompted JFK to write the book Profiles in Courage. When they voted to impeach they knew full well that this could very well be the end of their political careers. They put their country ahead of their careers and their political party and did so because it was the right thing for them to do! Thank you!

Ex-president Trump demonized each one of these senators by name during the CPAC rally on February 28th followed by a demand to each of their states to make sure they're primaried out and replaced in 2022.

The Articles of Confederation adopted in 1781 suggested a maximum of three terms for any delegate to prevent the abuse of power; the founders did not want the common relationship between the people and their representatives jeopardized. It took until 1990 for twenty three states to set term limits and in 1995, Chief Justice John Paul Stevens who had been nominated to the Supreme Court by the GOP wrote in his opinion that the Constitution did not grant these states the right to have term limits. Hogwash! That's the reason our founders gave us a Supreme Court full of Justices, to interpret the text of the Constitution along with all the associated documents leading up to the Constitution in order to re-interpret it over and over again until we got it right! I find it very peculiar Stevens didn't defer to what was written in the Articles of Confederation written in 1781 that suggested our representatives should serve no more than three terms. It seems Justice Stevens may have adopted a political position rather than an obvious juris prudence position, but isn't that what some of them do?

The founders were well aware of the human condition and knew many candidates would step forward and beguile the best of us into believing they too wanted this great experiment to work, when in fact, they were only focused on achieving power and self-aggrandizement that their elected offices would provide for them. The founders could only trust God and hope each generation had the spiritual and intellectual mettle that would enable them to select the best of the best from their fellow Americans that would enable us to continue to form a more perfect union, but this wasn't the case with the 130 members of the GOP caucus in Congress.

For sure, most of us Americans have not been using due diligence in the vetting and selection of our leaders which has ended up with us having more self-serving bureaucrats across the land than servants as was intended. These bureaucrats have beguiled their constituents into believing they have their backs, when in fact, their only goal has been to have a strangle hold on their elected offices. Few of them have any intention of ever crossing the aisle to compromise with their political opponents which means they do not have a stake in the union as was envisioned by the founders.

I hate repeating myself, but what is it that prevents some of us Americans from seeing what's been going on as being exactly what happened in 1930-35. History has shown us over and over again that when we make terrible choices, terrible consequences can follow. The German people turned their will and their lives over to Hitler and 10 years later every German city laid waste in ruins ... was divided into half with Russia taking one half and the allies caretaking the other half ... 6 million Germans, 6 million Jews, and 17 million other Europeans were dead. Those that were captivated by Hitler's spiel that his Third Reich was going to last for the next thousand years were nowhere to be found. Every country is destined for the same demise that doesn't believe history can repeat itself. The German people became so full or so sorry for themselves that they couldn't see the losing for the winning. This is what happens when citizens overlooked Hitler's dark mind and disturbing solutions that he promised were going to solve all their problems; and they bought it hook, line, and sinker! Ring a bell?

What epidemiologists feared most with this virus may have taken place with the arrival of two mutated strains; one from the UK and one from South Africa. The CDC is hopeful that the current vaccines in the pipelines will still prevent a person from getting either of these two strains, however, both strains are highly more transmittable and a bit more virile.

I still have not heard any recent CDC updates on what the risk of spreading the Covid virus through the HVAC systems in public buildings might be. Viral RNA has reportedly been found on air grilles and return air ducts on commercial HVAC systems, although detecting viral RNA alone does not imply that the captured virus was capable of becoming a transmittable disease. It would seem to me though that HVAC systems that lack .1 micron filters would re-circulate an airborne virus through the buildings infecting the people inside and making them carriers when they left the buildings.

....

January 6, 2020 will go down in U.S. history as America's day of disgrace! Trump stood on a stage out in front of the WH and began working hundreds of his supporters into a frenzy. He proclaimed the election was rigged, that he really won by a landslide, the election had been stolen from them, and that they were going to have to march up to the Capitol and fight if they wanted to save their country! They left and he continued tweeting claims that he won by a landslide and the election was rigged by the Democrats.

In a flash, his dream of holding an autocratic sway over this country came to roost ... Trump knew that what was about to take place would not have been necessary if he were re-elected. Well he wasn't and now he was between a rock and a hard place. He knew if he emboldened his supporters to storm the Capitol it would sit well with more than half of those that voted for him; disinformation he hoped would convince the rest. He may have even wished that he had made a move like this a year ago after he had not been impeached for withholding funds authorized by Congress for Ukraine , but he knew it was now or never, he had to seize the moment and he also knew this was the moment his supporters had been anxiously waiting for; he gave them the nod.

An estimated 8,000 insurrectionists made up of Trump supporters, white supremist groups, Nazi copy cats, Qanon members, and members of several militia groups overwhelmed the Capitol police, smashed windows, broke down doors, and rampaged into the Senate and Congressional chambers where the ceremonial vote tabulation of the electoral votes was in progress in both chambers; a young woman and four others were killed. They made their way inside the Capitol seconds after the representatives and senators of both houses stopped counting the electoral votes and made it to safe rooms. They even replaced the American flag on top of the Capitol building with a Trump flag. Some of the mob were heard yelling, "It's time for a civil war!"

The event in the Prattville movie theater twenty years ago confirmed once again that the clock for some of these insurrectionists had not moved one minute past the surrender at Appomattox Court House on April 9, 1865 as well; lots of unfinished business since then! The entire world watched in disbelief as the mob vandalized and desecrated both chambers, pilfered trophies to brag about later, and sat at the dais with their feet on the desk which they hoped would send a message to the world that this democracy here on this day in the U.S. was dead! It was an unspeakable and disgraceful tragedy that I and the rest of the world would never have thought possible.

Chapter 21

Further investigation revealed that GOP members of the House or Senate were seen escorting groups around the inside of the Capitol the day before and some of these same people were seen on camera the next day rampaging through the Capitol building. This suggested that the tour given the day before could have been a reconnaissance mission to obtain a layout of the building. What's even worse is a month has passed and the GOP Senate and Congressional caucuses have yet to condemn Trump for his part in the insurrection and invasion of our Capitol; it mustn't be their kind of bone to gnaw on like the Benghazi incident that happened in Libya. The GOP Senate back then conducted 17 hearings that they hoped would pin the blame on Hillary Clinton for the raid on our Embassy; it ended with Hillary Clinton being vindicated and exonerated.

Good news arrived during all this madness; the Georgia election supervisor announced that the Democratic candidates, Jon Ossoff and Raphael Warnock won the senate runoff election that was held the day before in Georgia. This was a sweet victory for the Democrats!

Immediately following the January 6th insurrection, Speaker of The House, Pelosi announced that Congress had begun impeachment proceedings and hoped they would take a vote to impeach as early as the following week; one week before the inauguration of Joe Biden. I was and still am not in favor of this because this in and of itself will incite more recriminations, acrimony, and political unrest across the nation which already is at a tipping point. We've proven time and time again that impeachment is not the tool to use to obtain justice because we are using politics to obtain justice when we should be using the law. Speaker Pelosi exposed her rancor for President Trump when she tore a copy of his speech in half immediately following his State of the Union message in January 2020. This was disrespectful and political maneuvering intended for the whole world to see. No matter what Madam Pelosi may think of Mr. Trump, I do not believe a criminal act such as inciting a crowd into insurrection deserves a political solution.

I would hope if the founders were able to return to review how Article 2, Section IV has worked thus far, they would opt to replace an impeachment trial of the president charged with high crimes and misdemeanors with a rule of law approach; not a trial by his political peers. However, if they remained firm and thought the president should continue to be judged by his political peers, I hope they would at least agree it should be done by a secret ballot. This would at least give them a chance to demonstrate as a body that their oath to the Constitution was more precious than their allegiance to their political party.

I keep on asking why there's not been a peep from any of Trump's supporters. Some say they're in denial which in and of itself is nothing more than sincere dishonesty! I choose to believe that they have always known he doesn't speak the truth; they just turn a blind eye to this behavior saying to themselves, "Who in Washington ever tells the truth?" This means there are never any facts in play, just a continuous flow of show and pretend and if this is the case, we're a lot worse off than I thought

Many of us including myself were not aware of Trump's disinformation and conspiracy messaging to the dark web sites via Infowars where they were re-packaged and re-sent to all the Trump supporters.

Alex Jones of Infowars began re-packaging everything from the 9/11 event to the Sandy Hook massacre with a conspiracy twist on the dark web that was unbeknownst to most Americans although millions of his followers across the land hung onto his every word. Roger Stone met with Alex years before the 2016 election to set the stage for Infowars to begin using Trump's conspiracy disinformation right after Trump declared he was going to run for president; the rest is history and most of us didn't see any of this coming.

The Russian interference in the 2016 election is beginning to make sense, especially when you see that Roger Stone was the go between the Russians, Alex Jones, and Trump. Stone's use of Infowars to ensure all the email addresses were given to Guccifer 2.0 which was the Russian GRU unit in charge of the hacking. This explains how the Russian GRU units knew exactly which Americans had been turned or played and sent them 120 million conspiracy ads on Hillary via the online media companies right up to the 2016 election.

The lack of any outcry across the land after January 6th from the GOP voters reinforces how indoctrinated these fifty million plus avid followers are that have swallowed all of Infowar's and Trump's lies. It is also clear to see how this moment of truth has affected our leaders. Some of them realizing too late that their turning a blind eye to these dark web sites to gain a favorable position with Trump has now become a threat to our democracy and it's not going to be easy to put any of them back in the box.

District of Columbia Prosecutor Michael Sherwin should have issued a citation to President Trump and cited him for sedition before he climbed aboard Air Force One heading for West Palm like the conquering hero on the morning of January 20, 2021. Any other leaders that were involved or were in any way complicit with the insurrection or violence on January 6th should also be made to stand before a judge in a U.S. Court of Law as would any other citizen suspected of these same criminal acts.

We've been telling the world that we are a country of law for 234 years and this is not the time to turn a blind eye to an ex-president or any other leaders or citizens suspected of sedition or abetting insurrectionists. These are capitol offenses that should be prosecuted and judged in a court of law, not in Congress or the Senate by their political peers who will be tempted to putting party before country!

What do you think an autocrat like Putin would do with any of his citizens that stormed the Kremlin? He'd jail every one of them without a trial in some far away Siberian gulag! This is the United States and they should be cuffed, made to stand in front of a judge while they are arraigned for the crimes of illegal entry into the Capitol, murder, and inciting insurrection against the United States of America. With respect to the president who may pardon himself, let the Supreme Court convene and settle this longstanding self-pardoning issue once and for all, but for sure, make sure he is made to stand and be charged in a court of law!

It's not the first time we Americans have raised up against our government and January 6th certainly won't be the last. There are some Americans in our country who have a different vision of what America should like and they are proving that they will go to any length to get there with or without democracy. Does this mean that there are 74 million Trump voters that are willing to switch from democracy to autocracy in order to retain white power? I don't know but it sure looks that way! Who would have ever thought voters in any congressional district would have sent a Qanon member like Marjorie Greene as their congressional representative to Washington DC? Who would believe with all the evidence to impeach Trump that the GOP would only be willing to censure him?

Hermann Hesse said it best, "The less able I am to believe in our epoch and the more arid and depraved mankind seems in my eyes, the less I look to revolution as the remedy and the more I believe in the magic of love." We're not there yet.

Mike Dowd, member of GW Bush's 2004 campaign suggests January 6th is really about a large number of Americans having issues with the line in the Declaration of Independence that reads, "... all men are created equal." He may be right and I'll bet some of the founders saw that one coming as well.

When I saw the mob rampaging through our Capitol buildings on TV, I saw two different sets of expressions that stood out on their faces. It was easy to see the tag along patsies who had been beguiled, played, and hoodwinked by Trump and then there were the intense driven expressions of the anarchists, insurrectionists, and militias that were demonical, almost savage who were hellbent on killing some of our leaders. This was more than a falling out by a few Americans. President Trump knew what made these people tick and he used them as pawns to take out his revenge on our system of government that was not letting him stay in power and hoping they would succeed. His followers may never fully understand what took place over the last four years, but the rest of us will. The good part about all of this is that We the people stood tall, our Republican and Democratic elected leaders did complete the count on the electoral ballots from each state, and we are going to have a new president proving that we have not let the government of the people perish. Slowly we will begin to get our bearings and we will come to see that some of these centrist anarchists were using Trump just as Trump was using them. They came out of the woodwork four years ago at Charlottesville never believing that their dark affair with Trump would end up with him giving them the green light to rampage through the halls of our Capitol four years later intent on overthrowing our democracy with his inspiration and blessing.

On the other hand, I understand how some people fall prey to conspiracy interlopers and I caution everyone not to assume that all the so called conspiracy theories that are out there are without some degree of warrant or credibility. Until now, I personally have not paid much attention to any of them. I mentioned earlier in this book about what took place when the Warren Commission was supposed to sift through all the evidence of the JFK assassination to determine exactly what took place in Dallas on that sunny afternoon on November 22, 1963. Most folks, especially those Texans that were in Dealy Plaza that fateful day, never believed a word of the Warren Commission Report because they knew otherwise and they also knew that the commission had arrived at an ending before they began hearing any testimony about the beginning.

Then there's the folks that do not believe the story the government released about what happened leading up to 9/11.

And let's not forget the Diebold conspiracy that took place during the 2004 election. A woman suspected foul play in the counting of the votes in Volusia, Florida and Cleveland, Ohio. She hired a computer programmer from Sweden who helped her prove her theory that the Diebold computers at those locations and maybe in other states as well during the 2004 election had in fact been programmed to change the vote tally when they were transferring the voting data from an election precinct to the main computer. HBO made a documentary that was pulled off the air after airing for a week; now who had that power!

I said before that I did not pay much attention to conspiracy theories which was a misstatement because I do remember paying attention to these three. I believe that our new president would be wise to prevail upon Angus King, IND senator from Maine to help set up a panel that could meet with these unbelievers to review and debunk some of these long standing conspiracies so as to make sure everyone has been heard. Nothing worse than our government having a smarter or holier than thou attitude on almost every major event when it doesn't ring true with the people. Senator Angus King suggests the government better start listening to the people if they want an all inclusive nation. He's right, if some of the people are not being heard they will damn sure find a way to get your attention.

Arthur Miller said, "The perfection of innocence, indeed, is madness." Who hasn't said, "I only did what anybody should have done." That doesn't hold any water for the overdevlopment of innocence contradicts our humanness and spiritual growth, and in this case, has impacted the lives of an entire nation. Those who attempt to destroy our democratic way of life because they feel righteous or worse, innocent, must be punished because feeling righteous or innocent are light years apart but still heinous undertakings with what happened on January 6th. Any nation that allows any type of political or national movements that are supported or promoted by disinformation, lies, or propaganda to flourish can only implode. We humans are societal and there is no way we can abide with one another if truth has been manipulated or set aside to serve a few. Any American that knowingly creates lies should not be allowed protection under the first amendment. Disinformation meant to undermine the public's faith in their government is sedition and should be punished to the full extent of the law.

Until Johann Guttenberg invented the printing press in 1439, the world was controlled by the powerful who created their versions of the truth and slew the naysayers who argued against them. For the first time in the history of mankind, the truth could be put into print and passed out to the peoples to read. It became the impetus for everyone to learn how to read and citizens began to have faith in humanity.

For six hundred years the daily newspapers throughout the world became and still are the leading force for printing the truth. Today we find ourselves in an environment where social media has almost replaced the newspaper and TV news spots to where most of the current generation here in the U.S. and around the world have never read a newspaper let alone looked to it for finding out the truth of what happened or who did what to who. They think of themselves as a somewhat sophisticated lot, gliding over the crowd, and a bit snobbish when it comes to what news trough they frequent to find out what they feel they need to know is going on in the world. This of itself is very dangerous for they unknowingly assume what they are learning is the truth which may not be the case. Remember, people become patsies when they set themselves up to become patsies. In many cases, the social media news outlets are delivering news content to users that fits their political persuasions. For others the news has been tweaked by the dark powers ever so slightly to where it's no longer the truth leaving the user completely unaware that they've been played. This has been going on since the beginning of mankind but never with such ease as it is today. The first newspaper casualties leading up to WW II were in , Italy, and Japan! In other words, the people in those nations thought they knew what was happening and were really the last to know what was happening because they had been played!

If half the people in America continue to source unsubstantiated versions of the truth it will only be a matter of time before democracy in our nation will fail because democracy cannot co-exist when suppressed with lies and disinformation. It will take strong leadership to ferret out those subversive and deceitful forces like Qanon, Infowars, and other underground news and media sources that create disinformation for a cause. It would be best to fight these kind of battles in a court of law than in the streets.

On February 23rd, the Senate convened a hearing to determine what exactly did happen that led to the Capitol being invaded and overrun on January 6th. It's clear to see the DEM party was trying to establish who was behind the uprising and the GOP party was trying to introduce messaging that suggests the crowd just got out of hand because of a few malcontents and there may not have been any malice aforethought which means nothing meaningful will come of this hearing. Anytime politicians or officials are convened to get to the truth on a matter that could involve their relationship with any of the subject matter it will be difficult for them to agree on anything much less the truth.

Trump convened a CPAC rally in Orlando wherein he drummed up his supporters, demeaned President Biden which ex-presidents try not to do, and inflamed his base into getting ready for the next election. The only words that came to mind looking at everyone there except Trump was they had no idea what this is doing to America. They're caught up in something they cannot let go of which is scary stuff!

With respect to Trump's part in what happened on January 6th, there's no doubt that he incited the mob to invade the Capitol and stop the electoral vote count. He was also instrumental in slowing up the decision to send the National Guard to the Capitol for three hours and if this proves to be the case, he should be charged in a court of law and receive the harshest of punishment if he is found guilty. The only way the truth can publicly become the truth will be for AG Garland to appoint a public prosecutor that has the power and full access to all the evidence, professional law enforcement agencies, intelligence data, and witnesses including everyone in Trump's cabinet.

Chapter 22

Let's get off the train at the next station, stretch our legs, and put all of what I've been talking about to one side until it's time to get back on the train for the final leg of our trip.

America for the most part is a Christian nation, and if this is so, this might be a good place where the believers and maybe even the non-believers can ask themselves, "What would the Master do?" There's a passage in Corinthians that talks about not being so spiritual minded that we are no earthly good. I interpret this to mean we best not walk around like we have it all together when we are not being of a maximum benefit to our fellows.

Two thousand years ago the people were no different from us today. They suffered miserably at the hands of the Roman occupation forces that wielded whips, prodded them with the tips of their spears, and executed them for not following their rules. Everyone was constantly looking for signs of the Messiah that the prophets promised would come. Jesus the Nazarene arrived on the scene and began healing the lepers, curing the sick, comforting the mentally ill, driving out the evil spirits from the possessed, raising the dead, and most of all, welcoming and commiserating with the sinners. He acted out of love and he knew the miracles were going to gain him a great deal of notoriety some of which would not set well with the Pharisees. All His followers were hoping He was the One and He would use His powers to destroy the Romans and declare himself King of the Jews. That's not what happened and it didn't take long for some of His followers to have mixed feelings about where He, His mission, and they were headed.

Fast forward 2000 years and nothing much has changed in the way we handle our disappointments, discouragement, and grudges. We who for the most part are living in the lap of ease, free to do what we want, and free to go where we want find ourselves in a continually agitated state!

Tennessee Williams summed it up best when he said, "All my life I been like a doubled up fist ... poundin', smashin', _ now I'm going to loosen these doubled up hands and touch things easy with them."

We all have our different sides, some of which are highly developed and some that are not developed at all. Our undeveloped sides prevent us from incorporating goodness, softness, kindness, thoughtfulness, and consideration into all of our everyday affairs vs poundin' and smashin' our way ahead.

Jesus knew the human condition and He spoke in parables which are teaching stories hoping this would help us to better understand what it is we each must do if we are to become a loving and caring part in God's Kingdom that he said was at hand! For three years He spoke to his disciples about being of service to everyone, serving one another, and yet, on the very night he was betrayed his disciples refused to let Him wash their feet. He had to pressure Peter to let Him wash his feet in hopes the rest of them would begin to understand the basics of what He meant by serving and loving one another. They just didn't get it and this had to have given Jesus pause as to where all of this was heading.

Hermann Hesse said, "If not for the beast within us we would be castrated angels." He too like millions of other Germans got caught up in Hitler's world in 1920 and rose in the Nazi party to where he was appointed Hitler's Deputy Fuhrer in 1937. In 1941 he flew solo to Scotland with hopes of negotiating peace. He was arrested, tried for war crimes, and sentenced to life in prison where he committed suicide in 1987. I believe he meant well but I'll bet that's not where he thought his life was going to take him. He had 46 years in prison to wonder how it was that he became so mesmerized with Hitler which is what happens when some of us patsies don't use our God given faculties to discern what it is that we are really getting into.

Find a quiet place and let John Powell, a Jesuit priest who wrote the book Unconditional Love in 1978 relate his version of the Prodigal Son.

There came the day when the doubters confronted Jesus and pressed a question they knew He couldn't answer safely; kind of what's going on in today's world don't you think? The crowd stood around him in a ring of hostility and posed the question, "What does God think of a sinner?" Jesus began to tell the Parable of the Prodigal Son. It was a story of a kind and loving father and his two sons. The younger son tells the father he wants his share of his inheritance and leaves without ever looking back. The father misses his son terribly and waits on the porch of the farmhouse every night, watching the road, praying for his son in hopes he'll return. Uncompassionate neighbors would stop by from time to time and let him know that his son was committing debauchery with every available or vulnerable women in town, acting stupid, and spending his inheritance like a fool..

Then one night, there on the porch his heart nearly explodes with excitement. He sees a figure coming down the road … he sees that it is his son. The father runs down the road, his heart pounding and his eyes filled with tears. Scripture scholars say that no father in that time would have run to his son as it would've been totally out of place. John Powell writes, "… it could only have happened to someone whose explosion of joy overcame all sense of time and social custom. The father hugs his boy tightly, huge racking sobs of joy shaking his body. Warm tears roll down his cheeks. The boy is saying something about not being worthy to come home as a son, and asking only to let him hire on as a field worker. The father hears nothing of this. His heart is saying: "I don't care where you've been or what you've done. All I care about is that you are home … you're home!" The father swallows hard, swallows the warm tears gathered in his throat, and calls for rings and robes and music makers. He orders the fatted calf killed and roasted over an open fire. This is a party to end all parties. "My boy is home!" When the older son comes in from the fields to discover the party going on in full swing he does not understand. He is angry; "You never gave a party for me and my friends." … "Oh, Son," the father says, "I understand. I love you so much. And I am so grateful for your faithfulness. You have stayed here with me. Everything I have is yours. Anytime you want a party for yourself and your friends, everything I have will be at your disposal. But there is something I must ask you to understand. Would you try to understand what goes on in the heart of a father when his lost child comes home?" The question hung there in the emotionally charged atmosphere.

This is one of the oldest love stories and everyone upon hearing it immediately see themselves in one of the three persons; the father, the prodigal son, or the other son." Just imagine standing there when Jesus looked into the faces of each person in the emotionally charged ring of accusers and said, "This is what God thinks of a sinner!" I don't know about you but tears were running down my cheeks when I read this in Powell's book. I didn't want to be seen as the other son or remember when I acted like the prodigal son when I was a young man, and for sure, I knew I had never been a very good father.

The disciples were always complaining to their Master that they were being mistreated by the Roman soldiers or the Pharisees to no avail because Jesus would tell them over and over again, "Submit!" or "You need to pray for your enemies". This is not what they wanted to hear! Things are not much different today although here we live in the richest country in the world, and yet, there are folks that have never ever expressed their gratitude for just being born here, much less anything else. There are stiff necks as well who will never accept submission as the solution to any of their grievances. Remember, many of the crowd that Jesus fed with loaves and fishes were yelling, "Crucify him" the following week. Kind of like how the mob decided to turn against their fellow Americans in our Capitol for that's how mobs behave.

Jesus was a Rabbi and Rabbis were teachers. He was trying to remind the crowds of their basic innate humanness ... what's really important in this world ... how the prodigal son's father's love for his son outweighed the gossip ... how the father was the salt of the earth ... the glue that was holding everything from truly coming apart ... the embodiment of goodness ... and his love and faith were immovable!

The prodigal son on the other hand had few to none of these qualities just yet ... he was biting at the bit to get out from under the supervision and doldrums of day to day farm life.

He took his inheritance and headed for the city to explore the delights of the world that he had only heard about; he was selfish and only thinking about himself. He never sent word to his father letting him know he was okay. He led an adulterous life, frolicked, and spent his inheritance. It was only after the money was gone and he was eating with the swine in a sty that he remembered the laborers on his father's farm lived better than he was living and he headed for home. He wasn't going home because he missed his father or brother; he returned home so he could have a place to stay, a warm place to sleep, nourishment, and time to think things out! How often does this play out in our society today?

The brother of the prodigal son was a mixed bag of human frailties, righteousness, and defects that most of us can identify with and would rather not look at let alone confess. Let's not forget; the parable was meant for each of us to see which of the characters in the story we could each identify with, and speaking for myself, it was the kindest of ways for me to come face to face of who I really am on this earth along with letting me see my woeful shortcomings and character defects.

....

The parable of the Good Samaritan left me feeling uncomfortable for there was an instance in my life when I was living in South America and passed by a stranger lying on a sidewalk bleeding from a head wound that haunts me to this day; I stepped over him and kept on going.

An expert in the law stood up to test Jesus, "Teacher," he asked, "what must I do to inherit eternal life?" ... "What is written in the Law?" Craftily he asked. "How do you read it?" Jesus answered, 'Love the Lord your God with all your heart and with all your soul and with all your strength and with all your mind and love your neighbor as yourself.' ... "You have answered correctly," Jesus replied, "Do this and you will live." ... But the man wanted to justify himself, so he asked Jesus, "And who is my neighbor?"

In reply Jesus said: "A man was going down from Jerusalem to Jericho, when he was attacked by robbers. They stripped him of his clothes, beat him and went away, leaving him half dead. A priest happened to be going down the same road, and when he saw the man, he passed by the man on the other side. So too, a Levite came to the place and saw him and passed by on the other side. But a Samaritan, as he traveled, came to where the man was; and when he saw him, he took pity on him. He went to him and bandaged his wounds, pouring on oil and wine. Then he put the man on his own donkey, brought him to an inn and took care of him. The next day he took out two denarii and gave them to the innkeeper. 'Look after him,' he said, 'and when I return, I will reimburse you for any extra expense you may have.'

"Which of these three do you think was a neighbor to the man who fell into the hands of robbers?" The expert in the law replied, "The one who had mercy on him." Jesus told him, "Go and do likewise."

I see these two stories as the crux for humanity and maybe the most important reason that Jesus came here. The expert in the law could not speak the word Samaritan because they were their enemies. Jesus knew some of us were somewhat spiritually minded, but he also knew that in and of itself didn't make us any earthly good. He was delivering a message that had to start from the bottom up. What good does it do us to have righteous opinions, achieve comfort, satisfaction, prestige, wealth, or power and then turn a blind eye to those on the bottom rung that can't begin to get a leg up on anything in this world. We forget that it's only by the grace of God that any of us are even here let alone what we each have or don't have in our lives, and yet, Jesus required us to help everyone and remind ourselves that we did nothing to deserve what we all have been given on the economic ladder of life; it was only the Grace of God that we had anything. He was letting them know that they could not keep what they had unless they gave it away and who wanted to hear that?

Virginia Satir said, *"What is obvious to me is that we did not create ourselves ... life is something inside of you. You did not create it. Once you understand that, you are in a spiritual realm."*

We are part and parcel of this Universe; we do not belong to ourselves. I have yet to meet anyone that said they planned on coming here. We are expressions of a Force that we cannot bring into view with our finite consciousness. It is all about goodness that we are here, we just have to learn not to be so frightened and not take everything so seriously which is the first step in discernment. Those of us that so often rush to attack or defend have no idea where they fit in and are always blaming everyone else for not having their way.

We happen to live in the richest and most powerful nation in the world, and yet, one would think from the way we live our lives and behave towards one another that we were on the verge of spiritual collapse and economic bankruptcy. Many of us have more of an investment in being separate than together.

Our Creator gave us one of the most beautiful planets in the Universe. The Hubbell telescope is a marvel and continues to send us unimaginable pictures of outer space that happened billions of years ago that some of us are not the least bit curious about. I cannot imagine what the billions of people that lived here before us would have given for a glimpse into the Universe. Why aren't we brimming with unbridled excitement and asking to see more as we wait for the news that we are not alone?

Our species began comingling with one another about 200,000 years ago and some of us have yet to accept all the different color variations and ethnicities that makes us all who we are today. In the last 900 years we've had 137 wars which proves our thinking will continue to be our undoing unless we all take a look at what's going on inside our minds and hearts.

World War II ended with the bombing of two Japanese cities because they would not surrender; two hundred thousand civilians were killed in an instant. The only reason we haven't had WW III is because our leaders know it will end with mutual destruction of ourselves, our enemies, along with the planet, and not because we're treating each other unkindly or that killing one another other is unacceptable. So, it's not a matter of trying to get this right as much as it is that we must get this right and it all begins with each one of us; there's no passing the buck! We will never get along with one another or have a lasting peace with the other nations in this world unless we accept and care for everyone, regardless of their color, religion, and ethnicity; everyone has a right to be here. We as a species must stop acting like we created this planet because we didn't; we are only here as guests and we've been improper guests for far too long and as long as we put all our trust in a peace backed by weaponry and intelligence, that peace will continue to elude us and our radical emotions will prevail.

We've been talking about many things throughout this book. There's an old Italian saying, "When the game of chess is over all the pieces go back into the same box." In other words, no one in our Creator's world is better or worse off in the grand scheme of humanity and it was no different 2000 years ago than it is today. If any of us think we are better than others we will all suffer the consequences. Again, we are not here to learn how to get along and care for each other; we are here to learn that we <u>must</u> get along and care for each other! Our history demonstrates the unimaginable costs for not having done so. The good news is, we will discover an unimaginable peace when we have learned to love and care for one another.

I found myself pondering the young soldiers from the South and the North who found themselves on the Gettysburg battlefield in Pennsylvania on the day before the battle pondering what was about to commence on that hot day on July 3rd, 1863. They surely knew this quiet place was going to turn into a killing field for them and their fellow Americans ... did some of them feel like they had been played ... maybe.

Democracy only works if everyone is paying attention to the bouncing ball; I am sure the Trump supporters that rampaged through our Capitol buildings will tell you that they haven't been played, and I'm sure they have not been paying attention to the bouncing ball which is why all this happened. People who have been played usually have no idea they've been played until it's too late and this a sad story in and of itself, and to make matters worse, people that have been played eventually are overcome with such shame and guilt, that they become dangerously morbid when they realize everyone but them knew they were patsies all along.

We need to put these past four years behind us but never forget what happened. A good way for this to begin is for each of us to go to a quiet place, close our eyes, take a deep breath, and ask our Creator to help us begin to start looking at each other, especially people of color with a new pair of glasses. Help us to see our part in all of this and to open our hearts and minds and become willing to embrace everyone regardless of their political persuasions or their less than honorable behavior, and to love and tolerate those with opposing ideas ... to ask Him every morning to reveal to each of us what we can do to help each other, and thank Him every night for our blessings before going off to sleep because that's what the Pilgrims did ... they knew if they continued to blame one another for everything that was going wrong they would all perish. So too did Abraham Lincoln know that we will all perish when he stood on the Gettysburg battlefield and said, "... that we here highly resolve that these dead shall not have died in vain -- that this nation, under God, shall have a new birth of freedom -- and that government of the people, by the people, for the people, shall not perish from the earth".

So, for the here and now, we need to remember that we are a part of the cosmos, we each are made of the same atoms that are in the stars, and we each are endowed by our Creator with certain unalienable Rights, that among these are Life, Liberty, and the pursuit of Happiness with which to fulfill our dreams. It is right for each of us to yearn and create an ideal life while we are on this earth, but it's most important that we know at a deeper level that we cannot do so alone; which means, for this to work, we must all work together under a canopy of love, trust, tolerance, and truth, and that's exactly what we have not wanted to do for the last 234 years!

If JFK were here today he might add, "We do this because this is hard."

T.S. Eliot said it best when he wrote, "We shall not cease from exploration. And at the end of all our exploring will be to arrive where we started and know it for the first time."

....

On the morning of January 21, 2021, President Trump left the White House for a farewell ceremony at 8 am at Andrews Air Force base before leaving for West Palm Beach. He could not bring himself to meet and extend well wishes to President Elect Joseph Biden, but we are told that he did leave a letter for him in the White House.

I was emotional when I watched some of the leaders from both parties leaving St. Matthew's Church in Washington DC after having attended Mass with Joe Biden and his family. It was so holy a moment to know that they thought attending Mass with him and asking God to bless them was indeed the best way they could begin the work that lay before them.

It's been two weeks since Joe Biden was sworn in and what a relief it is to see adults running our government again. The lies have stopped for the most part and daily news briefs have returned to solving problems not making them.

On February 13, 2021, the United States Senate as expected voted not to impeach Donald J. Trump. The GOP portion of the U.S. Senate proved once again that they have more of an allegiance to themselves, their party, and their constituents than they do for duty, honor, and country.

Georgia and Arizona began instituting sweeping new voting bills some of which will eliminate absentee and mail in ballots in the future elections. Arizona and Florida state senators have redrawn the boundary lines in their states that will all but eliminate the Democrats votes in some districts.

On March 22nd, a man armed with an Ruger 556 pistol modified with an arm brace killed nine shoppers and a 51 year old policeman in a grocery store in Boulder, Colorado. The shooter has been identified as a 21 year old male of Islamist decent who lived in a Denver suburb. His family says he was a disturbed individual who experienced delusional behavior.

The question we keep coming back to over the last 30 years is how does a mentally challenged or outright mentally disturbed person purchase or gain access to these efficient killing weapons that were intended to be used on a battlefield. Why are these weapons even available to the public and if they are allowed to be purchased by the public, why aren't there strict laws that ensure the person wanting to buy one of these automatic weapons has undergone a background check, be deemed mentally sound by a licensed psychiatrist, and be licensed by the state before this person can purchase and take the weapon out of the store amongst the public? At the very least, there should be a 72 hour waiting period before the weapon can leave the store or be taken possession of by a private party.

Every American knows the answer to these questions because we have been listening to this dribble for the last 30 years. The NRA is not so much an association for gun enthusiasts and hunters as much as it is a GOP lobby with 8 million members that will vote for any and all GOP candidates if those candidates will in turn ensure the NRA members they will be able to purchase, use, and transport these weapons for their personal use with no strings attached. So far, the GOP has kept their end of the bargain and the NRA has kept theirs by casting 8 million votes for GOP candidates in state and federal elections.

Seventy two percent of all Americans polled think our leaders should enact legislature to control who should be able to own these weapons. This doesn't add up because if all these people were being truthful, all these people would only be voting for candidates that wanted to enact gun control reform.

Ten people were shot down in a grocery store in Boulder, Colorado this past week. It's time we got honest with ourselves about this gun control business and stop acting so innocent when we think none of the 1300 people that have been killed over the last 30 years had anything to do with us.

We offer up a prayer with our condolences along with our sorrow for the families of the victims but never have I heard anyone say they might in any way be culpable or to blame for voting for the leaders that support the NRA gun lobby. Never have I heard a GOP leader express remorse for creating and enacting laws that led to these senseless acts taking place in the first place. Never have I heard any of my relatives, friends or co-workers ever express culpability for their part in any of these tragedies if they had voted for any of these leaders. We shroud ourselves in innocence when in fact we do have the power every time we're at the ballot box to elect leaders that will stop this madness! The citizens who continue to cast their ballot for leaders that support the NRA gun lobby that leads to men, woman, and children being slaughtered need to get honest!

Congressional Republicans are scheduled today to take a vote to remove Wyoming Congressional Representative Liz Cheney from her leadership post after she repeatedly accused Donald Trump for inciting the in insurrection on January 6th and disclaiming that he lost the election due to voting fraud. She has honored her oath to protect the constitution and for that she is a patriot.

Before closing, I want to remind you all of another extremely important issue, and that is, under no circumstances should our state or federal government instruct our teachers to promote or teach the pros and cons of any political party. Also, never should parents, our government, or our schools alter what has actually taken place in our history that would put any historical events into a more politically favorable or unfavorable light, such as, what has been taking place in Florida with Gov. DeSantis pushing his 'woke' policies; it's divisive for history should only be taught in the very context of what took place. Teaching politically crafted history is evil and one of the main reasons we are in the mess that we've been in for the last 234 years!

Our founders worried that some of our elected leaders wouldn't be able to let go of the power given to them by the voters, and with respect to President Trump, this was one of our greatest failings by those voters who chose to overlook his dark side which he ultimately used to try and keep himself in power. What's worse, many of our current elected representatives and senators are quite comfortable in the swamp that they were elected to drain which is another reason why the founders knew the voters could mess this great experiment up if they were unable to use due diligence and get honest when they voted.

Like millions of other Americans who found themselves with too much time on their hands after the Covid virus began, I decided to write a book about what had been going in America before and after Donald Trump was elected president in 2016. Maintaining a neutral position wasn't as simple as I thought it would be when describing what had taken place during the last four years that caused us to veer so far off the course from whence we began. Trump proclaimed a hundred times during his campaign that he was going to drain the swamp and here we are four years later with a swamp that is larger and deeper than when he began.

So, I decided that I would try and compare what the lay of the land was when the founders began and start from there. Once I did this I had a backboard with which to compare major issues, like who should or shouldn't be allowed to vote. The founders had a smaller swamp to deal with, but nevertheless, it was still a swamp. From there, I was able to skim through history and select what I thought were the most egregious and back sliding moments in our history that led to how we became who we are today.

I thank all of you that stayed on the train. I hope this narrative refreshed what were some forgotten but otherwise major events in our history, revealed some that should never have happened, some that happened for all the wrong reasons, some that happened and have never had closure to this day, and some that shed light on some of the events and tragedies that happened over the last four years that most of us wished had never happened.

The End

P.S.

I did send a letter to President Biden after he took office to see what he could do about replacing that stolen mailbox I mentioned on Page 139. I was hoping with his all his power that he would pass this on to one of the minions in his administration that would follow through and get the mailbox replaced. I did get a reply from one of his minions who failed to talk about the mailbox but did let me know much ado about nothing. As of this writing, the mailbox has not been replaced which saddens me for he must've forgotten one of the most important rules in becoming a leader which is … "It's the little things that really count and if you can't get the little things done, what good are you"?

A Final Commentary
William Falk
Editor-in-Chief The Week

It was an accident of history. On election night in 2016, Donald Trump's victory came as a shock even to him. As results came in, advisor Steve Banyon said, "Trump was speechless and 'horrified." Don Jr said his father looked like he'd "seen a ghost.." Like millions of Americans, Melania was crying, and they were not tears of joy. Trump's personal attorney, Michael Cohen, later said his longtime boss had told him the presidential run would serve as "the greatest infomercial in political history" – a way of promoting his real estate and reality – TV brand. Breaking news: Trump did not grow into the job. He tweeted, watched Fox, and golfed, turning the presidency into just another show. He used his platform and power to sow chaos, spout lies, and disinformation, poison our politics, defy norms and laws, pander to despots, alienate allies, downplay and actually worsen a raging pandemic that's killed 400,000 Americans, encourage and embolden white supremacists, incite an insurrection to overturn an election, and futilely try to fill his bottomless pit of narcissistic need.

It hasn't been good for the brand. In exile at Mar-a-Lago, he faces the real possibility that disgusted Republicans might convict him at a second impeachment trial. He may soon be hit with a barrage of state and federal criminal prosecutions for a myriad of potential crimes. His business empire lies in ruins, with massive debts coming due. Former aides and allies, including his once loyal Vice President Mike Pence, now shun him. He can't even tweet anymore – oh, cruel fate! In a perverse way, says Trump biographer Michael

D'Antonio, "this is the end that he would have scripted for himself." Trump has always seen himself as "a lonely hero" in a ruthless, Darwinian world, surrounded by enemies and backstabbing friends – besieged, betrayed, a victim fighting everyone to the bitter end. Donald Trump created his own dystopian reality, and we can now leave him to it.

A few thoughts & changes to consider:

1. Our Constitution may have been a gentlemen's agreement but that doesn't get us off the hook.

   It was vague … not legally explicit which tells me in some ways they were in a bind ... but they had a high degree of maturity, morality, trust, honor, and integrity than we do today. If they could pay us a visit, I don't believe they would use the Senate as a political remedy to resolve a criminal act by a president because they had to have known most elected senators would not have had the moxie to find one of their own guilty ... expediency left them little time to correct this wrong.

   So, this appears to be the same conundrum that the founders had in 1787 that ended with them taking the softer and fastest approach. The Senate will almost never convict a sitting president from their own party, so maybe it's finally time for the people to elect leaders the will create an impartial rule of law that will indict and impeach a president when Congress accuses a president of having committed a high crime or misdemeanor. This will prevent the president from being treated as if he or she is above the law and ensure that they are in fact not treated like a king. As it is now, even the SOTUS justices could be exacting out of revenge if they are of an opposing political party or acquit if they are of the same political party. Either way, the people lose.

   I suggest we devise a juror selection system whereby the jurors' identities are not disclosed. Each state will conduct a random juror selection process every year. Applicants will be citizens of the U.S., have no police record or court convictions, and three will be selected from each state when a president is elected. Their political registration will remain a secret. If a president is impeached, fifty jurors will be selected via a power ball like system and remain secret. A majority vote of 33 votes will be needed for impeachment.

An amendment needs to be added to the Constitution to prevent a sitting president from being above the law or pardoning himself or herself, otherwise he or she will be a monarch. If a president is accused of a crime by a citizen(s), the president should have to defend himself or herself in a court of law to a jury made up of its citizens.

2. Create an amendment that prevents SCOTUS from interfering with the will of the people after they have voted for a president. They must never interfere, override, or contradict the will of the people after they have cast their votes to elect a president as was the case when they set aside the Florida Supreme Court order to recount the Florida ballots in the 2000 election making it possible for GW Bush to be declared the winner. This should never be the case again. Ruth Bader Ginsburg said this was one of the Supreme Court's most shameful moments.

3. An amendment must be added or amended to the Constitution to ensure the president is in fact not above the law

4. All candidates for president must provide copies of their annual income tax forms for the last 15 years.

5. SCOTUS justice replacement(s) shall begin within 10 days after one of the justices has died.

6. No elected congress person or senate person sitting on a Congressional; or Senate intelligence committee is allowed to meet or discuss the information of the committee with anyone unless all the members of that committee give the nod.

7. Any candidate running for election or holding a local, state, or federal office must take an MMPI (Minnesota Multi-Phasic Personality Inventory) test every year to ensure they are of a sound mind, have no aberrant abnormalities, and have a fit mental capacity with no abnormal behavior that would compromise their duty or undermine the welfare of the citizens. All commercial and private pilots, law enforcement officers, judges and justices, ship and boat captains, and military personnel must take an MMPI test every year.

8. Enact an amendment wherein Congress must enact a law mandating a budget process where total expected tax revenues are equal to the expenditures and includes paying down a minimum of 7 percent

of the debt every year that includes taxing the
wealthy.

9. An impeached president must stand down until
judged not guilty by the Senate.

10. Under no conditions can a president authorize funds
or modify previously approved funds or spending
without approval of Congress

11. Under no circumstances can a president allow or
authorize fracking or mining in any state.

12. Amend the Constitution to read: the president may
not pardon himself and the VP who becomes
president may not pardon a president leaving office.
Nor may a sitting president pardon anyone in his or
her administration, congress, senate, or immediate
circle of associates or friends.

13. The president cannot pardon any person(s) that are or
were associated or involved with any ongoing
investigations involving the president.

14. A president cannot pardon anyone awaiting or
currently under indictment.

15. China is not an ally or our friend and therefor, should not be treated so. Congress needs to enact an espionage law directed at China to prevent Chinese students from going to U.S universities that have not been thoroughly vetted and extradite all Chinese espionage agents that are stealing our industrial, scientific, and space secrets as this is read.

16. The candidates for the office of the president, Congress, and the Senate must submit to take an MMPI test before they are qualified to campaign and an annual MMPI test every year they hold office.

17. The Electoral College will confirm the electoral votes from each of the states to Congress on Monday, December 12, which will finalize the 2020 presidential election. We need all agree that our Electoral College system needs to be modified, but I don't think done away with because it ensures the smaller states have a say in how our democracy works. The idea though that Electoral voters in each state could change the vote of the people in that state contradicts the intent of the system and nullifies the vote of the people..
The Party System allowed for each party to choose electors and this gave the electors the option to forego the people's vote and vote for their party's candidate; not what the Constitution allowed although there is little mention of this in the Constitution. The truth about us humans though is that if you give us an inch we'll take a mile.

The Supreme Court ruled in 1952 that state's parties can require the electors to pledge to vote for the parties nominee before they are sworn in as electors and the only reason they'd want to do that is quite obvious; the people's vote wouldn't matter. Some states used a secret ballot.

Various GOP factions including the president made over 60 attempts to overturn the election using the lower courts which were rejected and labeled frivolous. National polls now show 70 percent of the GOP voters back these baseless attempts as well.

18. We need an active 3 or 4 party system. Trump announced at his CPAC rally that he has no plans of starting a new party when he already is the leader and controls the Republican Party. There will be folks that may not want to remain in his party and will opt to cross over into the Independent Party which was meant to be a far right conservative party at its inception in 1967. So, if Trump is not going to start a new party, why don't the people of color or different ethnicities or anyone for that matter that have different ideas of what this country could like create their own 4th party in order to give themselves the representation that fits their needs. This would give us the makings for an active four party system wherein candidates from all four parties will be filling the seats in both houses making it necessary for all the members to have to cross the aisles and compromise. It's what the founders had in mind to bring about compromise because as of now we do not have a give and take proposition when it comes to both houses.

Acknowledgements

The Week Magazine – 1/29/21 . Editors Letter

Palya – Conf No. 5010673

Return from Tomorrow 26th Printing 1996

George Ritchie with Elizabeth Sherrill